Robert Williams Buchanan

The City of Dream

An Epic Poem

Robert Williams Buchanan

The City of Dream
An Epic Poem

ISBN/EAN: 9783744712903

Printed in Europe, USA, Canada, Australia, Japan

Cover: Foto ©Thomas Meinert / pixelio.de

More available books at **www.hansebooks.com**

G. Aitchison
12 May 1888

WORKS BY ROBERT BUCHANAN.

'The dumb, wistful yearning in man to something higher—yearning such as the animal creation showed in the Greek period towards the human—has not as yet found any interpreter equal to Buchanan.'—*The Spectator.*

'In the great power of appealing to universal Humanity lies Buchanan's security. The light of Nature has been his guide, and the human heart his study. He must unquestionably attain an exalted rank among the poets of this century, and produce works which cannot fail to be accepted as incontestably great, and worthy of the world's preservation.'
Contemporary Review.

POETRY.

COMPLETE POETICAL WORKS OF ROBERT BUCHANAN. With a Steel-plate Portrait engraved by ARMITAGE. One vol. Cr. 8vo. 7s. 6d.

SELECTED POEMS. With Frontispiece by THOMAS DALZIEL. 6s.

BALLADS OF LIFE, LOVE, AND HUMOUR. With Frontispiece by ARTHUR HUGHES. 6s.

THE EARTHQUAKE; OR, SIX DAYS AND A SABBATH. 6s.

PROSE FICTION.

Crown 8vo. cloth extra, 3s. 6d. each.; post 8vo. illuminated boards, 2s. each.

THE SHADOW OF THE SWORD.
A CHILD OF NATURE. With a Frontispiece.
GOD AND THE MAN. With Illustrations by F. BARNARD.
THE MARTYRDOM OF MADELINE. With a Frontispiece.
THE NEW ABELARD.
ANNAN WATER.
FOXGLOVE MANOR.
LOVE ME FOR EVER. With a Frontispiece by P. MACNAB.
MATT: A STORY OF A CARAVAN.
THE MASTER OF THE MINE. With a Frontispiece by W. H. OVEREND.

DRAMA.

POETICAL PLAYS. With a Note on the Modern Stage. [*In the Press.*

LONDON: CHATTO & WINDUS, PICCADILLY.

THE CITY OF DREAM

An Epic Poem

THE WAYSIDE

THE CITY OF DREAM

An Epic Poem

BY

ROBERT BUCHANAN

'The old creeds vanish, giving place to new:
Read here what paths God's pilgrims now pursue!'

LONDON
CHATTO & WINDUS, PICCADILLY
1888

[The Right of Translation is Reserved]

CONTENTS.

	PAGE
DEDICATION	ix
ARGUMENT	xiii

THE CITY OF DREAM.

BOOK I.
SETTING FORTH 1

BOOK II.
STRANGERS AND PILGRIMS . . . 27

BOOK III.
EGLANTINE 51

BOOK IV.
WITHIN CHRISTOPOLIS 68

BOOK V.
WITHIN THE GATE 87

BOOK VI.
THE CALVARIES 104

BOOK VII.
THE WAYSIDE INN 121

BOOK VIII.
THE OUTCAST, ESAU 141

BOOK IX.
THE GROVES OF FAUN 174

BOOK X.
THE AMPHITHEATRE 203

BOOK XI.
THE VALLEY OF DEAD GODS . . 222

BOOK XII.
THE INCONCEIVABLE 237

BOOK XIII.
THE OPEN WAY 271

BOOK XIV.
THE CITY WITHOUT GOD . . . 291

BOOK XV.
THE CELESTIAL OCEAN 334

L'ENVOI 359

INDEX TO THE SONGS.

	PAGE
Jesus of Nazareth	42
Mary Magdalen	44
'O child, where wilt thou rest?'	60
'Come again, come back to me'	91
'I have sought Thee, and not found Thee'	136
Proserpine	138
Song of Esau	154
'Kiss, dream, and die!'	175
'Black is the night, but blacker my despair'	231
'Dead man: clammy, cold, and white'	234
'Hark! I am call'd away'	245
'Little herd-boy sitting there'	252
'Where the buttercups so sweet'	253
'I am lifted on the wind'	266
'The woof that I weave not'	268
'Pleasant blows the growing grain'	274
'Forget me not'	350
L Envoi: 'O blessed Death!'	359

Dedication.

TO THE SAINTED SPIRIT OF JOHN BUNYAN.

O TELLER of the Fairy Tale Divine,
    How bright a dream was thine,—
Wherein God's City shining as a star
    Gleam'd silently from far
O'er haunted wastes, where Pilgrims pale as death
    Toil'd slow, with bated breath!

Like children at thy knees we gather'd all,
    Man, maiden, great and small;
Tho' death was nigh and snow was on our hair,
    Yet still we gather'd there,
Feeling upon our cheeks blow sweet and bland
    A breath from Fairyland!

The sunless Book, held ever on thy knee,
    Grew magical thro' thee;
Touch'd by thy wand the fountain of our fear
    Sprang bright and crystal clear;
Thy right hand held a lily flower most fair,
    And holly deck'd thy hair.

Of Giants and of Monsters thou didst tell,
    Fiends, and the Pit of Hell
Of Angels that like swallows manifold
    Fly round God's eaves of gold;
Of God Himself, the Spirit those adore,
    Throned in the City's core!

O fairy Tale Divine! O gentle quest
    Of Christian and the rest!
What wonder if we love it to the last,
    Tho' childish faith be past,
What marvel if it changes not, but seems
    The pleasantest of dreams?

Far other paths we follow—colder creeds
    Answer our spirits' needs—
The gentle dream is done;—'neath life's sad shades,
    The fabled City fades:—
The God within it, shooting from his throne,
    Falls, like a meteor stone!

So much is lost, yet still we mortals sad
    Despair not or grow mad,
But still search on, in hope to find full blest
    The City of our quest;—
New guides to lead; below, new lights of love,
    And grander Gods, above.

And while of this strange latter quest I sing,
    First to thy skirts I cling
Like to a child, and in thy face I look
    As in a gentle book,
And all thy happy lore and fancies wise
    I gather from thine eyes.

Tho' that first faith in Fairyland hath fled,
    Its glory is not dead;
And tho' the lesser truth exists no more,
    Yet in thy sweet Tale's core
The higher truth of poesy divine
    For evermore shall shine.

There dwells within all creeds of mortal birth,
    That die and fall to earth,
A higher element, a spark most bright
    Of primal truth and light;—
No creed is wholly false, old creed or new,
    Since none is wholly true.

Wherefore we Pilgrims bless thee as we go
    With feeble feet and slow;
Light of forgotten Fairyland still lies
    Upon our cheeks and eyes;
And somewhere in the starry waste doth gleam
    The City of our Dream!

ARGUMENT.

ONE Ishmael, born in an earthly City beside the sea, having heard strange tidings of a Heavenly City, sets forth to seek the same; and as he fares forth he is blindfolded by Evangelist, and given a Holy Book; reading which Book, he wanders on terrified and blindfold, until, coming by chance to the house of one Iconoclast, he is relieved of the bandage covering his eyes, and led to an eminence, whence he beholds all the Pilgrims of the World. Quitting Evangelist, he encounters Pitiful, and is directed towards the City of Christopolis, but in the crowded highway leading thitherward he meets Eglantine, who warns him that Christopolis is not the City of his quest. Yet nevertheless he proceeds thither in his new friend's company. He wanders through Christopolis and sees strange sights therein; but being denounced for unbelief and heresy, he takes refuge beyond a great Gate dividing the City into two parts. Wise men accost him and warn him that peace and assurance are to be found only in the Book given him by Evangelist; but this in his perversity he denies, and casting away the Book is again denounced as unbelieving,

THE CITY OF DREAM.

BOOK I.

SETTING FORTH.

IN the noontide of my days I had a dream,
  And in my dream, which seem'd no dream at all,
I saw these things which here are written down.

And first methought, with terror on my heart,
I fled, like many a pilgrim theretofore,
From a dark City built beside the sea,
Crying, 'I cannot any longer bear
The tumult and the terror and the tears,
The sadness, of the City where I dwell;
Sad is the wailing of the waters, sad
The coming and the going of the sun,
And sad the homeless echoes of the streets,
Since I have heard that up among the hills

There stands the City christen'd Beautiful,
Green sited, golden, and with heaven above it
Soft as the shining of an angel's hair;
And thither comes not rain, or wind, or snow,
Nor the bleak blowing of Euroclydon,
Nor moans of many miserable men.'

Now in my dream meseem'd that I had known
A melancholy neighbour, old and blind,
Named Faith, led by a beauteous snow-white hound,
Named Peace; and this same Faith, grown worn
    and weak
With wandering up and down the weary ways,
Had one day learn'd, high up among the hills,
Strange tidings of the City Beautiful,
And heard in sooth a far-off melody
Of harps and lutes, blown from the heavenly gate.
Now, when he spake of this, upon his face
There grew a gleam like moonlight upon water,
Sweet with exceeding sadness; and at last,
Though blind, he had left his lonely home again,
And stolen across the valleys silently
At midnight; and he had return'd no more.

Him, after many melancholy days,
And many wrestlings with a darkening doubt,

Setting Forth.

I, Ishmael (lone descendant of a race
Who chased the mirage among desert sands),
Follow'd in fear; and lo! I fled with speed
Like one who flees before some dreadful beast;
But just beyond our town I met with one
Clad in white robes and named Evangelist,
Who, at the threshold of his summer dwelling,
Girt round by plenteous harvest, sat and smiled;
To whom I cried:

'O thou who sittest here
In thy fair garden girt by golden glebe,
Instruct me (for thy beard is white and wise)
Which is the pathway to the heavenly City
Call'd Beautiful, first of the Land of Light?'

Then said Evangelist, with courteous smile:
'O Pilgrim, close thine eyes, and wander on;
One Faith precedes thee, blind, led by a hound,
Else trusting God; and when thou stumblest, rise;
And when thou comest among thorns and flints,
Praise God and pray; and when in some deep
    slough
Thou flounderest, bless God and struggle through.
But chief, be warn'd, to walk with close-shut eyes
Is safest, seeing our twin eyes of flesh

Mislead us, and a thousand evil things
Are made for our temptation. Grant me grace;
And I will give thee this brave Book to read,
And for the further safety of thy soul
Will bind this blessèd bandage o'er thine eyes,
To keep thy sight from evil. Though thine eyes
Be blind from seeing *forward*, ne'ertheless
Look *down* thou canst while wandering, and glean
The wisdom of the Book.'

                              A space I paused,
Gazing into his coldly happy eyes,
Then cried: 'But *thou?*—O master, answer me!—
Art *thou* content here in the dales to dwell,
Nor climb thyself the heavenly heights whereon
The wondrous City stands?'
                                Then with a smile
As soft, as still, as is the snake of fire
Coil'd up and flickering on some happy hearth,
Evangelist replied : 'My post is here,
Not on the mountains, nor a rocky place;
He whom I serve hath given me this my task
To blindfold pilgrims and to point them on;
This house is His, this porch with roses hung,
These golden fields; nor can I quit my post
Until He sends His own dark Angel down.'

And on my head methought Evangelist
Placed his soft hands in blessing; and my soul,
With one long sigh, one glance at the blue heaven,
Assented; and methought Evangelist
Did blindfold me, and set me on my way,
And place the Book within my hands to read,
Then softly singing in the summer sheen,
Cried, 'Courage!' as I wander'd from his sight.

And as I wander'd on, not seeing whither,
But trusting in some heavenly hand to guide,
I, casting down my gaze upon the Book,
Read these things, and was little comforted :—

In six days God the Lord made heaven and earth,
And rested from His labours on the seventh;
Dividing firmament from firmament,
Fishes He made, and flesh, and flying birds,
And, lastly, Man; next, from a rib of Man,
Woman. These twain He in a garden set,
Naked, and glad, and innocent of heart;
But in the centre of the garden placed
A Tree for their temptation. Thither came
The ancient snake upon his belly crawling,
And bade the woman pluck the fruit and eat.
And first the woman ate, and then the man,

And knew their nakedness, and were ashamed;
And furthermore an Angel with a sword
Drave them from Eden into the sunless waste.

From these twain had the generations come,
The million generations of the earth,
Bearing the burthen of that primal sin;
And whatsoever man is born on earth
Is born unto the issues of that sin,
Albeit each step he takes is predestined.

Further, I read the legend of the Flood,
Of Noah and of the building of an Ark,
And how the Maker (as a craftsman oft
Rejects a piece of labour ill begun)
Destroy'd His first work and began again
With sorrow and the symbol of the Dove.

Much, furthermore, I read of the first race
Of shepherds, Abraham's race and Jacob's race;
And of the chosen people God deliver'd
Out of the land of bondage. Portents burnt,
Strange omens came, wild scenes and faces flash'd
Before me, and I ever seem'd to hear
The rustle of the serpent; till I heard
The voice of David cursing to his harp

His enemies, and smiting hip and thigh,
And holding up his blood-stain'd hands to God.

And ever across my soul a vision flash'd
Of a most direful Form with robes of fire,
A footfall loud as many chariots,
A voice like thunder on a mountain-top,
And nostrils drinking up with joy divine
The crimson sacrifice of flesh and blood;
And ever as I read I felt my soul
Shake with exceeding fear, and stumbled on
With fleeter footsteps; and I fled for hours
Ere, with a fascination deep as death,
I cast my gaze upon the Book again.

And now I read of pale and wild-eyed kings,
Of sounding trumpets and of clarions,
The clash of hosts in carnage, and the shriek
Of haggard prophets standing on the heights,
And urging on the host as men urge hounds;
As in a mirror, darkly, I beheld
The generations drift like vapour past,
Driven westward by a whirlwind, while on high
The Breath Divine like fire came and went;
And, suddenly, the storm-cloud of the world
Uplifted,—there was light—stillness and death;

All nature lay as one vast battle-field,
And cities numberless lay desolate,
And crowns were strewn about and broken swords,
And everywhere the vulture and the raven
Pick'd at the eyeballs of slain kings and churls;
And through the world a crimson river of blood
Ran streaming, till it wash'd the feet of God.

These things I gather'd, trembling like a leaf,
And moaning, 'God of Thunder! save my soul!
Destroy me not, Destroyer! Pity me,
O Pitiless, but let Thine anger pass!'

And now, methought that I had left my home
Behind me, and was far beyond the town,
When, suddenly, I heard upon my path
A crowd of people hearkening to one
Who raised his voice aloud and prophesied.
'Who speaks?' I ask'd; and one, with low, deep laugh,
Said, 'Only our old prophet, Hurricane:
He began early, and the people applauded;
But now the matter hath outgrown his wits,
And newer lights are risen.' Whereon I said:
'Methinks I know the man; he hath a house
Within a suburb of our town, and ever

He mocketh all his neighbours and the poor,
And praises only God, and priests, and kings.'

And in my dream I heard him, Hurricane,
Railing aloud to those who flock'd around:

' Scum of the Maker's scorn, what seek ye here?
Go, thou whose sin is black, and kiss the lash;
Haste, thou whose skin is white, and strike for kings.
O miserable generation, foam
That flashes from the Maker's chariot-wheels,
What do you crave for, shrieking for a sign?
See yonder o'er your heads the sun and stars
Hang like bright apples on the Eternal Tree,
And day comes, and the night is wonderful,
And æon after æon, 'spite your groans,
The eternal Order stands. What seek ye, worms?
To shake away the slime of that first curse,
Spoken when ye were fashion'd out of dust?
It is the mission of the worm to crawl;
No snake is he, and cannot even sting
The heel that bruises him. Crawl on for ever;
Obey your masters here and yonder in heaven—
Ye cannot slough your sin or quit your curse.'

Then a voice deep and rough, as from the throat
Of some strong wight, responded:

'Softly, master!
What profit comes of railing? We who hear,
An we were worms indeed, might creep and die;
But being men, we deem thy counsel blind,
And all thy words as impotent as sparks
Blown by the bellows from my smithy fire.
Nay, those thou bidst us honour are (I swear
By Tubal Cain, the founder of my craft!)
The plagues of this green earth. I know them well,
I rate them, I! the monsters of this earth,
Blind priests and prophets blind, and blindest kings,
And conquerors slaying in the name of God.'

Then Hurricane made answer, while a groan
Went through the inmost ranks of those who heard:
'I tell you, ye are dust of evil, things
For mighty powers to work with. God is strength,
His blessing makes strong men, and they are strong
Who blister you and bind you to your doom,
Black slaves and white. Worms, do ye rave of
    rights?
I tell you, He who fashion'd you for pain,
And set you in a sad and sunless world,
Scatters your rights as the eternal sea
Loosens the fading foam-bells from its hair.
What man cried out, "There is no God at all?"

I swear to you, by sun, and stars, and moon,
By hunger, by starvation and disease,
By death, that there is God omnipotent,
Awful, a King, a strong God! yea, indeed,
The Maker of the whirlwind and the worm,
The judgment waiting in the heavens o'erhead,
The vengeance burning in the earth beneath,
The end of sin, the doom no man eludes,
Not even at the very gates of death!'

Now in my dream I shudder'd, for methought
I heard the living echo of the Book;
So, sick and sad at heart, I turn'd away,
And hasten'd, desolate, I knew not whither.

Methought I wander'd on and on, for long,
Shadow'd with sorrow, smitten through with sin,
Not heeding whither, blindfold, caring not
If the next step of my sad pilgrimage
Should be into some nameless, open grave.
But as I crept across the darken'd earth,
O'er which the sad sky shed a sobbing rain,
One cried to me, 'Poor soul, take shelter
    here!'
And following the summons of the voice
I felt the cold touch of an outstretch'd hand,

Which led me darkly through an open door,
Up steps of stone, into some unknown dwelling.

Then said I, pale, blindfolded, Book in hand:
'Who spake? whose hand was that which led me
    hither?
And what strange dwelling have I enter'd in?'
And sharper, shriller than an eunuch's voice
One answer'd, ' But for that same blinding band
Across thine eyes thou for thyself couldst see —
Perchance, good man, my name is known to thee,
Iconoclast, — called sometimes " Gibe-at-God,"
Whose name hath travell'd over the wide earth.'

Then all my spirit darken'd for a moment,
For I had heard the name said under breath
With Satan's and with Moloch's and with Baal's,
And my young soul had loathed the man who
    mock'd
All that the world deems holy. But as I stood,
Troubled and timorous, he did laugh aloud,
Saying:
        ' My name hath reach'd thee, I perceive,
And, though thou deem'st it evil, I have hope
To gain thy good opinion presently . . . .
Whence dost thou come? and whither dost thou go?'

The Pilgrim.

I come from yonder City beside the sea,
And seek the Beautiful City of the Lord.

Iconoclast.

And dost thou think to gain that City's gate
(If such a city there be, which travellers doubt)
Blindfolded, with that bandage on thine eyes?

The Pilgrim.

Yea, verily; for a good man set it there,
Evangelist.—But wherefore dost thou laugh?

Iconoclast.

O foolish Pilgrim, wherefore did thy Lord,
Whoever made thee, or receives from thee
Credit for having made thee, give thee sight,
If thou consentest not to look, or see?

The Pilgrim.

I know not. These are mysteries. Yet I know,
Evangelist did bid me journey thus.

ICONOCLAST.

I know the fellow, a fat trencher slave,
He wears no bandage, he, nor goeth forth
On pilgrimage, but sitteth in the sun,
Right prosperous, and eyes his golden glebe.
O fool, to be persuaded by this priest
Out of thy birthright; to be blind and dark;
The sun to see not, or the stars and moon,
Or any light that shines; to turn thy face
Into the tomb of dead intelligence;
To quit mortality and be a mole!

THE PILGRIM.

My townsman, Faith, precedes me: he is blind,
And yet he journeys safely through the land.

ICONOCLAST.

Leave faith to Faith; since the good, simple soul
Is eyeless, let his other senses thrive!
But *thou* hast eyes, and eyes were given thee
To see with; that to doubt, were blasphemy!

THE PILGRIM.

Why should I see? This Book held in my hand
Assures me 'tis a miserable world,
Base, burthen'd, and most bleak to look upon.

ICONOCLAST.

See for thyself! Wherefore consult a Book
Upon a point of eyesight? Look, and see!

THE PILGRIM.

I dare not. I am stricken dumb and sad,
After the testimony written here.

ICONOCLAST.

If there be misery in the ways thou treadest,
If this thine earth be wretched and unclean,
It is because so many walk in blindness,
And read the dreary gospel written there.

THE PILGRIM.

How may that be? God fashion'd all things well;
And only by man's sin did all grow sad.

ICONOCLAST.

Assuredly; God fashion'd all things well.

THE PILGRIM.

And all had still been well had man not eaten
The bitter Tree of Knowledge, and been shamed.

ICONOCLAST.

Softly, good friend; that is the one good tree
Adam ne'er tasted, not to speak of Eve
Or any wiser woman. Cast that Book
Over thy shoulder! Leave the dreary dream;
Forswear the apple and the fig-leaf; cease
To credit fables old of fire and flood;
Quit gloomy visions and crude eastern nights
Of legendary horror: in a word,
Cast off thy bandage and thine ignorance,
And look abroad upon thy destiny!

So saying, with one quick movement of his hand,
Iconoclast did snatch from off my brows
The bandage placed there by Evangelist;
And lo! I scream'd, and with my trembling fingers
Cover'd mine eyes, then, trembling like a leaf,
Perused the stranger's face, and saw it full
Of many wrinkles, and a snake-like sneer
Playing about the edges of the lips.
And it was noon, noon of a cold grey day,
A silvern, melancholy light in heaven,
All calm, the prospects and the distances
Sharp and distinct to vision, but no sun.

'Where am I?' next I murmur'd; and, 'Behold,'
Answer'd that other, 'on an eminence
Thou standest, named Mount Clear; for all the air
Is crystal pure, and hither rise no mists.
Follow me higher; far above my dwelling
I have built a solitary garden-seat,
Commanding a great prospect o'er the earth.'
Methought I follow'd, and we gain'd the height,
And, full of wonder now, I look'd abroad.

I saw great valleys and green watery wastes,
Deep-shelter'd woods and marshes full of mist,
And rivers winding seaward; then, mine eyes
Following the winding rivers, I beheld,
Far away, silent, solemn, grey, and still,
The waters of the Ocean; and thereon
Sat, like a sea-bird on the ribbèd sand,
A City that I knew to be mine own;
But following the windings of the coast
I beheld other Cities like mine own,
All hungrily set beside the wash of waves,
Looking expectant, seaward; and from each
Came solitary figures as of men,
Mere specks upon the highways and the fields,

All toiling, as it seem'd, with constant feet
To those green slopes whereon I stood at gaze.

Then as I look'd, and wonder'd, in mine ear
The old man murmur'd : 'Lo, thou lookest on
The Cities of the Nations of the Earth,
Each crouching by the sad shores of the Sea
Infinite, dreadful, mighty, without bound ;
And in each City thou dost look upon
A different legend and a different God
Lengthen man's misery and make him mad ;
Further, from City unto City have gone
Tidings of that same City Beautiful
Thou seekest ; at the gate of each there sits
An arch-priest, like thine own Evangelist,
Blindfolding those who wearily set forth ;
And these, the Pilgrims thou beholdest now
As specks afar, go stumbling sadly on ;
And if they perish not upon the way,
As ninety-nine in every hundred perish,
Hither among the hills of ironstone
They, slowly ascending, by such hands as mine
Are of their blinded ignorance relieved.'

Whereat I cried, in bitterness of heart :
'I see, but seeing comfort find I none,

But all thou showest me is sick and sad,
For lo! the things I fled from, the sad Earth,
The melancholy City, the grey Heaven,
And the vast silence of the unfathomed Sea!'
And turning to Iconoclast, I cried:
'Thy words are shallow, and thy counsel blind!
Lo! thou hast snatch'd the bandage from my eyes,
And I perceive the fables of the Book;
What shall I do, and whither shall I go?'

'Haste homeward!' smiling said Iconoclast;
'Back to thine earthly City, work thy work,
And dream of Cities in the clouds no more.'

But with a moan, uplifting hands, I cried:
'Whither, oh whither? To return is Death,
For mine own City is dreadful, and the Sea
Hath voices, and the homeless winds of woe
Wander with white feet wearily on the deep;
And every slope beside the sea is green
With the dead generations; and I seek
A City fairer and not perishable,
Peaceable and holy, in the Land of Light!'

Then did Iconoclast, with bitter scorn,
Cry: ''Tis an infant moaning for the moon,
For the moon's phantom in the running brook.

O fool! there is no City Beautiful
Beyond these Cities of the Earth thou seest!'

But turning now my back upon the Sea,
And on my native City, I beheld
A mighty land of hills. There, far away,
Beyond the pastoral regions at my feet,
Beyond the quiet lanes and wayside wells,
Rose mountains, darken'd by deep woods of pine,
With air-hung bridges spanning cataracts,
And rainbows o'er the waters hovering;
Mists moved, celestial shadows came and went,
While higher, dim against the blue, there rose
Peaks soft as sleep, white with eternal snow.

'What land is *that*?' I question'd; and the other
Answer'd: 'I know not; nay, nor seek to know;
For those be perilous regions, with an air
Too thin for man to breathe; yet many, I wis,
Have travell'd thither (O the weary way!),
But never a one hath hither come again.
And how they fared I know not, yet I dream
That never one doth reach those frigid heights,
But on the crags and 'mid the pathless woods
They perish, and the skeleton hands of Frost
Cling to them, breaking up their bleaching
    bones!'

But now I cried: 'O fool that I have been
To talk with such a shallow soul so long!
A scoffing voice like to the mocking-bird's,
The dreary echo of a hollow sound
Bred in an empty heart. For, lo! I see
The land afar, and, though the ways be dire,
Thither I fare, since, far among the heights,
Beyond the scoffer's voice, beyond these vales,
Beyond the weary wailings of the sea,
First in its place the Heavenly City stands!'

So stood I trembling in the act to go,
When grey Iconoclast, with cynic sneer,
Not angry, cried: 'Stay yet!—I had forgot!
Not far beyond these valleys lies indeed
A City wondrous smiling to the sight
Like that which thou art seeking. In its streets
Full many a prosperous pilgrim findeth peace.'
And, smiling bitterly, as if in scorn,
He added: 'O'er the mighty earth its fame
Hath travell'd on four winds! Who hath not heard
Of this same City of Christopolis?'

Then I upleapt i' the air and waved my hands.
'The name! the name!—He built it with His blood!—
I charge thee on thy life, point out the way!'
'Thou canst not miss it,' said Iconoclast;

'For if the milestone or the finger-post
Should fail thee, only seek the open road,
And there beshrew me if thou meetest not
With many of its priestly citizens,
Who will direct thee onward willingly.
Still, if thou lovest wisdom, be advised —
Turn back and hasten home. Christopolis,
Methinks, is *not* the City of thy quest.'

'How knowest thou that?' I cried, full eagerly.
'Hast thou thyself fared thither?'
                                    'Verily,'
Answered the greybeard; 'more, within its streets
I first drew breath!'

THE PILGRIM.
                I understand thee not.
Born *there*, and yet, alas! thou sittest *here?*

ICONOCLAST.
I could not choose. She from whose womb I came,
More mighty than my yet unwoven will,
Would have it so!—and thus on golden streets
I ran, and under golden fanes I played,
And in the splendour of Christopolis
I fed and throve, till, weary of so much light,
While yet a fleet-heel'd boy I fled away.

The Pilgrim.

Fled? From thy birthplace? from thy happiness?
O fool, to quit the paths and ways of peace!

Iconoclast.

I was not peaceful in those peaceful ways,
I did not love my birthplace. So I fled.

The Pilgrim.

Was it not fair?

Iconoclast.

    Most fair.

The Pilgrim.

        And holy?

Iconoclast.

            In sooth,
My nurses said so much.

The Pilgrim.

      Yet thou art *here!*

Iconoclast.

I loved my freedom better far than fanes:
Within those scented shrines I could not breathe.

Besides, the people were idolaters,—
Fools of the fig-leaf, blind inheritors
Of that sad symbol of a slaughter'd God.
I left them, and I came to warn the world
Against the follies I had left behind,
Or haply now and then with this weak arm
To aid some miserable human thing
Their citizens have hunted even hither!'

He added, with a strange and inward smile:
'Go thither, if thou wilt—seek out its gates—.
Remember that I warn'd thee 'twas in vain.'

More might his lips have spoken garrulously,
But swiftly down the silent heights I ran,
Thrusting the Book into my breast; and now
Methought my soul was wroth against the man,
Iconoclast. Most fleet of foot I fled,
Until I reach'd the shadowy vale below,
Through whose green heart there wound a dusty
    way
Where many men and women came and went.
But as I leapt a brook to gain the road,
Suddenly on mine ears there swept a sound,
A tumult, then a tramp of horses' feet,
Sharp yelp of hounds, and all the cries o' the chase.

Wondering I stood, and lo ! across the meads,
There came a naked man who shriek'd for dread,
Speeding as swift as any dappled deer;
And close behind him silent blood-hounds ran,
Swiftly, with crimson nostrils to the ground ;
And after these came a great company,
Priests in red robes, and hoary crownèd Kings,
And pallid Queens with grey and golden hair,
With countless savage slaves that ran afoot,
And huntsmen, shrieking, ' In the name of God !'
And much I fear'd the hounds behind the man,
Lolling their crimson tongues to drink his life;
And lo ! they would have caught and rent the
    man,
But, suddenly, he sprang with one swift bound
Over the threshold of a house of stone,
A lowly place white-visaged like a shrine,
That at the corner of a little wood
Stood with a spire that pointed up to heaven.
Therein he leapt and vanish'd through a door
That stands for ever open ; and the train
Were following when there rose beneath the porch
A figure like an angel with one hand
Outreaching; and they dare not enter in,
But with a sullen roar, clashing like waves,
Broke at the threshold, foam'd, and were repell'd.

Then, gazing past the Spirit, I beheld
A chancel and an altar, and the man,
With panting mouth and wild eyes backward gazing,
Cast prone before the altar, faint with fear;
And further, full of wonder, raising eyes,
I read these words written above the porch—
'Iconoclast hath built this church to God!'

Then did I pray and weep, crying aloud:
'Lord, let me judge not, since Thou art my Judge,
For I perceive an angel bright doth guard
The Temple of the Scoffer, and the same
May be Thy servant, though his place be set
Outside Thy City, in a rocky place.'
Then turning, I gazed upward, and behold!
On the cold eminence above my head,
I saw Iconoclast in milk-white robes
Walking with sunlight on his reverent hair;
And as he walk'd upon the golden sward
He scatter'd seeds and call'd, and many doves,
That rear'd their young beneath his lonely eaves,
Came fluttering down in answer to his call,
Making a snow around him, and were fed.

BOOK II.

STRANGERS AND PILGRIMS.

AND now my path was on a public road,
   And where I walk'd methought the weary air
Was full of lamentations ; for the sick
Lay on the roadside basking in the sun,
The leper with his sores, the paralysed
Moveless as stone, the halt and lame and blind,
And many beggars pluck'd me by the sleeve,
And when I fled shriek'd curses after me ;
And my tears fell, and my knees knock'd together,
And I fled faster, crying : ' That first curse
Still darkens all ! Oh, City Beautiful,
Where art thou ?—for these ways are sad to tread.'

Even as I spake I heard a gentle voice
Close by me saying, ' Good morrow, gentle Sir ;
'Tis sweet and pleasant weather ;' and I cried,
Quickly, not looking in his face who spake:
' I am in haste, and cannot pause for speech—
Farewell !' but, lo, the other touch'd my arm,

Saying: 'One word, I prithee, ere thou fliest.
In yonder village, Poppythorpe by name—
Pastor I dwell—my name is Pitiful.
I know thine errand. Prithee, since 'tis late,
Accept the shelter of my roof this night.'

THE PILGRIM.

I cannot rest. A wind behind me blows,
And like a cloud I travel darkly on.

PITIFUL.

And whither away?—Stay, from thy wayworn face
I guess;—thou goest to Christopolis?

THE PILGRIM.

Again that name. Oh help me! Guide me thither.

PITIFUL.

Most gladly. But, if thou wilt trust in me,
Rest for to-night, to-morrow fare afresh;
From hence the City is a weary way.

THE PILGRIM.

God help me!—I would fain not rest at all
Until the hunger of my heart is fed.
But tell me of those wretched on the road?
Whence have they come, and whither do they go?

Pitiful.

Those wretched are but Pilgrims like thyself—
They, too, are crawling to Christopolis.
Ah, look not on them, or thy heart may fail—
For few will ever gain the golden Gate.

Then all my force was broken, and I leant
Heavily on the arm of my sad guide,
A pale tall wight with soft eyes red from tears,
And through a wicket gate across the fields
We pass'd, and came unto a lowly house,—
A peaceful house beside a running rill;
And Pitiful did bring me food and milk;
And Sentiment and Sensibility,
His two grave daughters, made me up a bed
Deep, soft, and drowsy; that same night, methought,
I slept therein; upon the morrow morn
Rose languid, and went forth upon my way.

The road was busy still with eager folk,
Coming and going, but I saw them not,
For I bethought me of the blessèd Book,
And drew it from my heart, and as I walk'd
I read its solemn pages once again.

And now I read a tale so sad and sweet,
That all the darker matter of the Book
Dissolved away like mists around a star.
And I forgot the thunders of the Word
Spoken in Sinai to the bloody tribe,
Seeing a white Shape rise with heavenly eyes
By the still sleeping Lake of Galilee—
And Him, that Shape, the sick, and halt, and lame,
The miserable millions of the earth,
Follow'd in joy; and by His side walk'd women,
Tall and most fair, fair flowers that grew 'mong
    thorns
Like to the Hûleh lily; and the earth
Blossom'd beneath the kiss of His bright feet.
But, suddenly, out of the gathering cloud
Above the footsteps of that Man Divine,
Jehovah's eyes, bloodthirsty, terrible,
Flash'd at the pallid, patient, upraised face;
And He, the Paraclete, the Son, the Lamb,
Trembled and held His hand upon His heart,
Crying: 'O God, My God, if it may be,
Have mercy on Me, do not shed My blood!'
Whereon, methought, before my sight there swam
A vision of a night sown thick with stars
Like leopard spots, the deep dead dark below,
The flashes of the torches round a town,

And the shrill sound of that last victim's shriek
To an omnipotent and vengeful God.

Now as I read, methought I stopp'd mine ears,
And fled in horror from the thoughts that surged
Within mine own sad soul; and all the earth
Seem'd hateful to me, yea, the scent of flowers,
The savour of the new-mown hay, the breath
Of browsing sheep and kine, all odour of life,
Grew sick and sacrificial; yea, mine eyes
Shed tears like blood; and my soul sicken'd, saying:
' How should this God have mercy upon men,
Seeing He spared not His anointed Son?'

Aloud I spake in agony of heart,
And as I ceased there came unto my side
One clad in crimson, bearing in his hand
A snow-white staff; and Time upon his hair
Had snow'd full long, but in his jet-black eyes
There burn'd a bitter and a baleful light.
'Peace!' cried he, lifting up his wand on high:
'Peace—thou blasphemest!'
      Starting like a thief,
To have my thoughts so angrily surprised,
I gazed into the other's angry face
In question, but, ere yet my lips could speak,

That other, sinking lower his shrill voice,
Proceeded:
            ' What art *thou*, that thou shouldst judge
The cruelty or mercy of the Lord?
A Pilgrim, by the hunger in thy face—
Perchance a Pilgrim to Christopolis?
Nay, silence yet—and pluck not at my robe—
My guess was right, and to Christopolis
Indeed thou farest; thank the Lord thy God
They heard thee not who ope and shut the Gate,
Else surely would they never let thee in.
For less than thou hast harbour'd in thy heart
We hunted down a human wolf last night,
And would have slain him as a sacrifice,
But that an evil spirit interposed!'

Then did I tremble, for in him who spake
I recognised one of that hunting train
Whom I beheld upon the level meads
That hour I parted from Iconoclast.
Wherefore my heart woke in me angrily,
And in a low and bitter voice I said,
' I saw that chase,—and blest the holy form
Who from your cruelty deliver'd him.'

White as sheet-lightning flash'd that other's face,
And his voice trembled crying: ' Once again

Thou dost blaspheme! He did deny God's justice,
And God in justice gave him to our hands.'

'Nay then,' I answered, 'God, for such a deed,
Was much too pitiful.'

'Fool!' the other cried,
'Did yonder semblance cheat thee?' Did thine eyes
Fail to perceive that yonder seeming shrine,
Erected by accurst Iconoclast,
Was but the brilliant-colour'd mouth of Hell?
And did Iconoclast (for I perceive
Thy lips have talk'd with that arch-enemy!)
So cheat thy vision that thou knew'st him not
For what he is, black Belial and a fiend?
I tell thee, though his hair be white as snow,
His face most holy, sweet, and venerable,
He is the procurer of Satan's self;
And those white doves thou saw'st around his head
Devils attendant, taking from his hand
The crumbs of guile, the seed of blasphemy!
His spell is on thee yet—his seal is there,
Over thine eyelids,—down upon thy knees,
Pray God to shrive thee from thy hateful sin
Of that dark speech with the abominable,

And even yet thy sinful soul may see
The light and glory of Christopolis.'

Then spirit-shaken, broken, and appall'd,
Part by the horror in the stranger's eyes,
Part by the dim and darken'd memory
Of what my soul had read within the Book,
I cried aloud, and fell upon my knees,
And o'er my head the multitudinous clouds
Took dark and formless likenesses of One
Down-looking in His wrath; and as I pray'd,
I did remember how Iconoclast
Had blacken'd and reviled the Holy Book,
And wickedly blasphemed the very God.
Wherefore I moan'd: 'Forgive me, Holy One!
By Thy Son's blood forgive me, for I knew not
With what false tongue I spake.'
       Then to my feet
Uprising, tottering as one drunk with wine,
I still beheld the stranger watching me
With cold, calm eyes. 'What man art thou?' I
 cried,
'How shall I know that *thou* too art not false,
Some devil in disguise?'
      Full scornfully
The other smiled. 'By this same garb I wear,

And by this wand I wave within my hand,
Know then my priestly rank and privilege.
My name is Direful, and high-priest am I
Within the Holy City, where I preach
God's thunders and the lightnings of the Cross.
And if thou askest humbly, with strong sense
Of thine own undeserving, I perchance
May help thee through the golden City's Gates.'

'Thou!'—cried I—'*thou!*' then with a sob I
  said,
Clutching the pallid priest's red raiment-hem,
'Is it not written that those Gates stand wide
To all whose souls are weary and would rest?'

'To all whose souls are weary of their sin,'
The other said, 'and seek to glorify
His name who built the City with His blood.'

THE PILGRIM.

O pole-star of our sleepless sea of pain—
Still shines He there?

DIREFUL.

   Whom meanest thou?

The Pilgrim.

      Christ the King!

Direful.

He reigns for ever through His deputies,
Christ's Vicars, Servants, and anointed Kings—
These to His glory day and night upraise
Hosannahs, building with their blessed hands
Temples, and fanes, and shrines of purest gold.
There mayst thou, as a fringe upon the skirt
Of His bright glory, hang for evermore,
Swayed into rapture by each heavenly throb
Of that divine and ever-bleeding Heart,
Which even as a raiment weareth those
Who do partake its glory and believe.

The Pilgrim.

Ah me! if this be sooth, what shall I do
To win such rapture and deserve the same?

Direful.

Deserve it thou canst never, but perchance,
Thine own iniquities remembering,
Thou yet mayst win it. First, mark well—this gift
Comes from no merit and no power of thine,

Who, if God used thee after thy deserts,
Would now be trembling in eternal flame,
Or 'neath His heel be crushed to nothingness!

The Pilgrim.

What have I done to merit such a doom?

Direful.

Done?—sum it in two little words—*thou art*.

The Pilgrim.

If that be sin, God made me, and I am.

Direful.

God, in His mercy, suffers thee to crawl
As He doth suffer worms and creeping things;
God, in His justice, might obliterate
Thee and all creatures living from the earth.

The Pilgrim.

Not so; that duty the created owes
To the Creator, the Creator, too,
Owes the created. God hath given me life,
I thank my God if life a blessing is,
How may I bless Him if it proves a curse?

DIREFUL.

Fool! juggle not with words, lest the red levin
Fall down and blast thee. Rather on thy knees
Crave, as a boon, from the All-Terrible,
What thou mayst ne'er solicit as a right.

THE PILGRIM.

I pray! I pray! Father, Thou hear'st, I pray!
Nay, have I not by gracious words and deeds,
By holy living, love for all my kind,
Pray'd to and praised, loved goodness for Thy
    sake?

DIREFUL.

Nay, neither words, nor deeds, nor love avail—
They are but other names for vanity—
Only believe and thou mayst gain the Gate.

THE PILGRIM.

Instruct me further. What must I believe?

DIREFUL.

In God Triune, yet One—in God the Father,
In God the Son, and God the Holy Ghost—
In God's eternal Book, and in His Church;
In God's fair City, builded under Heaven,
And rear'd upon the hundred thrones of Hell!

The Pilgrim.

Why not? Belief is easy. Only show
The City and its Gateway, and I swear
No soul shall flout me for my lack of faith!
Yea, take me to divine Christopolis—
Let me be sure that shining City *is*—
Let me upon its fair perfections gaze—
And I will own indeed so blest a place
Transcends my best deserving, and will thank
That gracious God, who made me what I am,
For giving me this precious gift of life!

Thus speaking we had wander'd slowly on
A little way upon the dusty road;
But now behind us, riding hastily
There came that glorious hunting company
Which sought to slay the lonely hunted man.
And unto him who spake with me there strode
A slave, who held an empty-saddled steed
Bitted with gold and bright caparison'd;
Him Direful beckon'd, then to me he turn'd,
Crying, ' Fare forward!—there beyond the hill
Lieth the shining City of thy quest.'
So saying, lightly to his seat he sprang,
And in the track of that same hunting throng
Prick'd on his eager steed.

            Then, sighing deep,
I gazed around me, on the weary way
Strewn with the weary and the miserable,
And every face was lighted with the flame
Of famine; yea, and all like bloodshot stars
Shone forward the one way; but ah! the limbs
Were feeble, and the weary feet were sore,
And some upon the wayside fell and moan'd,
And many lay as white and cold as stone
With thin hands cross'd in prayer upon their rags.
Meantime there flash'd along on fiery wheels
Full many a glorious company which bare
Aloft the crimson Cross, and mighty priests
Glode by on steeds bridled with glittering gold,
And delicate wantons on white palfreys pass'd
With soft eyes downcast as they told their beads,
And few of these on those who fell and died
Look'd down, but seem'd with all their spirits bent
To reach the golden Gate ere fall of night—
Only the priests stoop'd sometimes o'er the dead,
And made the hurried sign o' the Cross, and went.

Now as I gazed and sicken'd in despair,
Because my force within seem'd failing fast,
I met two glittering upturn'd eyes
That from the wayside grass regarded me;

And lo! I saw, upon two crutches leaning,
A cripple youth with gold hair like a maid's,
A pale face thin as is a skeleton's,
And thin soft hands, blue-vein'd and waxen white;
And pitiful and weak he would have seem'd
But for the light within his eyes, which shone
Most starlike yet most baleful, fraught with flame
That ne'er was kindled in a vestal shrine.
He meeting now my gaze of wonder, smiled,
And such a smile wear wicked elfin things
That in the lustre of the moonlight live
And dance i' the starry dew. 'Well met,' he cried,
In shrillest treble sharp as any bell,
'Well met, good Pilgrim! Stand a space, I pray,
Yea, stand, and buy a song.'
      Then did I mark
He bare within his hand long printed strings
Of ballads, and, as ballad-singers use,
Stood with his arms outreaching and intoning
Praise of his wares.
     'I prithee, Pilgrim, buy!
Songs of all sorts I carry—songs for maids,
For sucking souls, for folks on pilgrimage,
Songs of Satanas and of Christ the King—
Come, buy, buy, buy; for with the thrift o' the
  sale

I hope betimes to buy myself an ass,
Mounted whereon, full gallop, I may gain
The golden Gates, nor rot upon the road
With those who fare a-foot.'

      And, while his eyes
Gleam'd wickedly and merrily, he clear'd
His throat, and in an elfin voice he sang :—

JESUS OF NAZARETH.

Tomb'd from the heavenly blue,
 Who lies in dreamless death?
  The Jew,
Jesus of Nazareth!

Shrouded in black He lies,
 He doth not stir a limb,
  His eyes
Closed up like pansies dim.

The old creeds and the new
 He blest with his sweet breath,
  This Jew,
Jesus of Nazareth!

His brows with thorns are bound,
 His hands and feet are lead;
  All round
His tomb the sands stretch red.

Oh, hark! who sobs, who sighs
  Around His place of death—
    'Arise,
Jesus of Nazareth!'

O'er head, like birds on wing,
  Float shapes in white robes drest;
    They sing,
But cannot break His rest.

They sing for Christ's dear sake;
  'The hour is here,' each saith;
    'Awake,
Jesus of Nazareth!'

Silent he sleeps, thorn-crown'd,
  He doth not hear or stir,
    No sound
Comes from his sepulchre.

'Awake!' those angels sing;
  'Arise, and vanquish Death,
    O King!
Jesus of Nazareth!'

Too late!—where no light creeps
  Lies the pale vanquish'd one—
    He sleeps
Sound, for His dream is done!

Tomb'd from the heavenly blue,
Sleeps, with no stir, no breath,
The Jew,
Jesus of Nazareth!

Some stood and listen'd, others cross'd themselves
And hurried past, one shriek'd out, 'Antichrist!'
And as he ceased a troop of hooded forms,
Women black-stoled, with crosses in their hands,
Passed swiftly by, and some at him who sang
Glanced sidelong, laughing with a sign obscene;
Answering that sign the cripple sang again:—

MARY MAGDALEN.

I saw in the Holy City, when all the people slept,
The shape of a woeful woman, who look'd at heaven, and wept.

Loose o'er her naked shoulders trembled her night-black hair;
Her robe was ragged and rent, and her feet were bleeding and bare.

And, lo! in her hands she carried a vessel with spices sweet,
And she cried, 'Where art Thou, Master? I come to anoint Thy feet.'

Then I touch'd her on the shoulder, 'What thing art thou?' I said;
And she stood and gazed upon me with eyes like the eyes of the dead.

But I saw the painted colour flash on her cheeks and lips,
While she stood and felt in the vessel with tremulous finger-tips.

And she answer'd never a word, but stood in the lonely light
With the evil of earth upon her, and the darkness of death and night.

And I knew her then by her beauty, her sin and the sign of her shame,
And touch'd her again more gently, and sadly named her name.

She heard, and she did not answer; but her tears began to fall,
And again, 'Where art Thou, Master?' I heard her thin voice call.

And she would have straightway left me, but I held her fast, and said,
While the chill wind moan'd around us, and the stars shone overhead,

'O Mary, where is thy Master? Where does He hide
    His face?
The world awaits His coming, but knows not the time or
    the place.

'O Mary, lead me to Him—He loved thee deep and
    true,
Since thou hast risen to find Him, He must be risen
    too.'

Then the painted lips made answer, while the dead eyes
    gazed on me,
'I have sought Him all through His City, and yonder in
    Galilee.

'I have sought Him and not found Him, I have search'd
    in every land,
Though the door of the tomb was open, and the shroud
    lay shrunk in the sand.

'Long through the years I waited, there in the shade of
    the tomb,
Then I rose and went to meet Him, out in the world's
    great gloom.

'And I took pollution with me, wherever my footsteps
    came,
Yea, I shook my sin on the cities, my sin and the signs of
    my shame.

'Yet I knew if I could find Him, and kneel and anoint His feet,
That His gentle hands would bless me, and our eyes at last would meet,

'And my sin would fall and leave me, and peace would fill my breast,
And there in the tomb He rose from, I could lie me down and rest.'

Tall in the moonlit City, pale as some statue of stone,
With the evil of earth upon her, she stood and she made her moan.

And away on the lonely bridges, or on the brink of the stream,
The pale street-walker heard her, a voice like a voice in a dream.

For, lo! in her hands she carried a vessel with spices sweet,
And she cried, 'Where art Thou, Master? I come to anoint Thy feet.'

Then my living force fell from me, and I stood and watch'd her go
From shrine to shrine in the daylight, with feeble feet and slow.

And the stars look'd down in sorrow, and the earth lay
    black beneath,
And the sleeping City was cover'd with shadows of night
    and death,

While I heard the faint voice wailing afar in the stony
    street,
'Where art Thou, Master, Master? I come to anoint
    Thy feet.'

Then said I, creeping close to him who sang,
'God help thy folly! Surely thou dost frame
Lays for mad moonlight things, not mortal men
Who soberly on holy business fare,
Seeking the solemn City——' In my face
The cripple laugh'd, then with forefinger lean
Outstretching, and his great eyes glittering,
He cried, 'Who prates of moonshine? He who
    seeks
The moonshine City?'
                        Then I turn'd away,
And with a darken'd face was passing on,
Much anger on my heart, when, suddenly
Sinking his voice, while his great eyes grew fill'd
With tearful dew, the singer cried, 'Fare on!
God help *thee*, brother—God make sure for thee
The City of thy dream!'

                        My sad soul stirr'd
By that new tone of pity in the voice,
I paused again, and, on the crippled form
Glancing in wonder and in tenderness,
Said, 'I have strength, and I shall gain the Gate!
But *thou?*'
            Again the cripple's lineaments
Changed into wickedness and mockery,
And loud he laugh'd, as shrill as elfins laugh
Seated in fairy rings under the moon,
And elfin-like he seem'd from head to foot,
While on his cheek and in his lustrous eyes
The pallid moon-dew gleam'd. 'Hie on!' he
        cried;
'Fly thou as fast as any roe, be sure
That I shall reach that ne'er-discover'd bourne
As soon as thou!'
                Thereon I turn'd my back
And set my face against the steepening hill;
And, as I climb'd among the climbing folk,
I heard the cripple's voice afar behind
Singing a weird and wondrous melody;
And even when I heard the voice no more
The sound was ringing in my heart and brain,
Like wicked music heard at dead of night
Within some fairy circle by the sea.

But still I fared with never-faltering feet,
Nor rested, till I gain'd the height and saw,
Far down below me, strangely glittering,
A valley like a cloud, and in its midst
A shining light that sparkled like a star.

BOOK III.

EGLANTINE.

NOW, presently I saw the countless spires
　　Like fiery fingers pointing up to heaven,
And 'neath the spires were gleaming cupolas,
Columns of marble under roofs of gold,
Netted together in the summer haze,
And lower yet, like golden rivers, ran
The streets and byways, winding serpentine.
Still was the heaven o'erhead, and sunset-lit;
One white cloud, pausing like a canopy,
Enroof'd the wonder of a thousand domes.

And now the highway that my footsteps trod
Grew populous, and every face was set
Towards the hot sunshine of the shining walls;
And lo, methought, with joy, ' At last I see
The City of my dream !'

　　　　　　　　　Even as I spake,
The river of life upraised me, surging back

To let a glorious company sweep by,
And struggling in the stream I recognised
Another hunting throng like that which sought
To feast its hounds upon the naked man:—
Kings in their crowns, Queens in their golden hair,
Priests in red garments, filleted with gold,
Huntsmen with hounds, and couriers that a-foot
Ran crying, ' Way there! in the name of God!'
Beneath the fierce tramp of their horses' hoofs
Some fell, and groan'd; they paused not, but swept
    on;
And after those were vanish'd with a blare
Of trumpets, into the far City's gate,
Came other trains as shining and as swift,
Until mine eyes were dazzled utterly.
Then, casting eyes on those surrounding me,
Many in rags I saw, who shriek'd for alms,
And some that sturdily strode on with wares,
Others that danced and sang, and others still
That dragg'd their feeble limbs along in pain.
But here and there, with crosses sewn in silk
Upon their bosoms, walk'd mysterious men,
To whose long skirts the halt and maim'd did cling,
Though still they heeded not, but in a trance
Walk'd on with eyes upon the far-off spires.
Then did I wonder, looking eagerly

For one of friendlier aspect than the rest
Whom I might question; but each man I mark'd
Seem'd struggling forward with no other thought
Than how to gain the shining shelter first.

Swept onward swiftly in mine own despite,
As in a sultry sea I gasp'd for breath,
Until, the highway widening as it went,
I saw upon its side a grassy knoll,
Whereon, down-gazing at the passing folk,
Sat one most strangely dight in Eastern wise,
With robe and caftan girdled round his waist,
His feet bare, in his hand a leafy branch.
A wight he was of less than common height,
With world-worn face, and eyes suffused with dew
Of easy tears, but when he spake his voice
Was like a fountain in a shady place.
Now, as he spake, some laugh'd, and others cursed,
Shaking their clenchèd fists into his face;
But most went by unheeding and unseeing.
But, as two ships made in the self-same land,
Although they meet amid a fleet of sail,
By some strange signal or mysterious sign
At once do know each other and exchange
Kind greetings in mid-ocean, so it chanced
That I and this same curious wayfarer

Finding our eyes meet suddenly together,
Smiled kindly on each other unaware ;—
And though I ne'er had seen the face before,
Methought 'Thank God, at last I find a friend'—
So struggling from the throng, with elbow-thrust,
Amid the cries and blows of those I push'd,
I fought my way unto the stranger's side.
Him did I greet, and instantly he smiled
A brother's answer, and full soon we stood
In gracious converse, looking on the throng
That like a river roll'd beneath our feet,
And on the glistening celestial towers.

STRANGER.

A mighty company ! and each one there
Bearing his own dumb hunger in his heart.
God grant they find the loving cheer they seek
In yonder City ; but, in sooth, I fear
It is too small to feed so many mouths.

THE PILGRIM.

O tell me—for I hunger to know all—
And thou of that same City art, methinks,
A happy and a blest inhabitant ;
See I God's City ?—Name its name to me,
For I have dream'd it over many years.

STRANGER.

Thou seest the City of Christopolis.

THE PILGRIM.

Rejoice!—the sweet name echoes in my heart!—
It is indeed the City of my dream!

STRANGER.

Be not so sure.   All those who journey thither
Conceive the same until they enter in,
But, having enter'd, many exchange their mirth
For lamentation, even as *I* have done.

THE PILGRIM.

Thou dwell'st there?   Thou dost know it?   'Tis thy home?

STRANGER.

Home have I none—even as the field-mouse makes
Her brittle dwelling in the fallow-field,
Alone, unfriended, houseless I abide—
There's not a door in yonder shining place
Would open to receive me; not a space

In the necropolis that stands hard by
Wherein my weary bones might find a grave.
I went there, and I sought a refuge, friend;
The glimmer of the gold-heaps dazzled me,
And I crept out upon the open earth.

THE PILGRIM.

What curse is on thee, then?—what blight of
    sin?—
Thou art not tainted? Even if thou art,
Repent, and be forgiven, and enter in.

The stranger smiled, and somewhat bitterly,
With petulant ring in his low voice, replied:—
'I have repented; but 'tis not my sin
That makes me exile from Christopolis.
Long years ago, a melancholy Man,
Who went abroad and wrought in love for men,
Was crucified upon the very spot
Where stands the midmost Church and inmost
    shrine.
This place a desert was in those old days,
But of that martyr's seed hath sprung like wheat
This golden harvest of a thousand spires;
And by his name the City is called, and now

The hosts within it hail the martyr'd " King,"
Yea, " King of Kings, Almighty, Very God,"
And drag to death and direful punishment
All heretics who kneel not at his tomb.
Now mark me, though I love his memory,
Because of his abundant charities,
And still the more because they martyr'd him,
I will not give to any man of earth
The worship I reserve for very God.'

Whereat I cried, 'Blaspheme not! Thou dost
    speak
Of Christ the King! Wilt thou not worship
    Him?
Oh, look on yonder glittering domes and spires,
Those shining temples of a thousand shrines,
He built them all!—He made this blessed home
For pilgrims, yea, He built it with His blood!
Yet in thy folly thou denyest Him!'

So saying, with mine ever-hungry eyes
Fix'd on the far-off flame, I hurried on,
Moving in haste along the quiet knolls.
The other follow'd, keeping pace with me.
And still the wonder of the City grew,
While all my soul in rapture drank it in,

Till pausing, dizzy with mine own delight,
Panting, with hand held hard upon my heart,
I cried aloud,
    'Oh, yea! It is indeed
The City of my quest! So great, so fair,
I pictured it, a miracle of light.
Dost thou not bless the hand that fashion'd thus
A haven where all weary souls may rest?
Aye, call Him God, or King, or what thou wilt,
Dost thou not bless Him for this wondrous work
Which in itself betokens Him divine?'

I ceased; but with a sudden wail of pain
The other threw his arms into the air,
Crying, 'Though golden in the light of day,
And all enwrought it be with earthly gems,
Thy sepulchre, O murdered Nazarene,
Is still thy sepulchre!' and, suddenly
Turning upon me with a fever'd face,
He added, 'Even as wondrous faery gold,
Gather'd in secret by a maiden's hand,
Turneth to ashes and to wither'd leaves,
So shall that City soon become to thee.
Christ's City, sayest thou? Christ's? Christopolis?
If that be Christ's I call my curse on Christ
Who built it to profane humanity!'

Then shrank I from his side, as one that shrinks
From tongues of fire, and, horror in mine eyes,
Gazed at that other, greatly wondering;
And as I stood, a pilgrim hastening by
Cried out, 'Avoid that man! It is a snake!
He speaks for thy perdition!'
       Suddenly
The stranger's face grew calm, the wind of
  wrath
Pass'd from it, leaving it as sweet and bright
As still seas after storm. Upon his heart
He press'd his hand, saying, 'Forgive me,
  friend,
How should *my* curse avail?' and, lo! I thought,
'I will not leave him for a little yet—
Perchance my faith (for, ah! my faith is great,
Beholding now the very City's walls)
May lead him from the dolour of his ways.'

And soon, methought, we twain together moved
By secret paths across the open fields
To the fair City; and the paths we took
Were almost solitary, for the throng
Of pilgrims kept the great and dusty road.
Green were the fields with grass, and sweet with
  thyme,

And there were silver runlets everywhere
O'er which the willow hung her tassell'd locks,
And song-birds sang, for it was summer time,
And o'er the grass, in green and golden mail,
The grasshoppers were leaping, and o'er head
A lark, pulsating in the warm still air,
Scatter'd sweet song like dewdrops from her
    wings.

And now, albeit we had not turn'd a step,
But held our eyes still on the golden Gates,
The City seem'd more faint and far away,
Lost in the golden tremor of the heat.
For as we went, from flowery field to field,
I seem'd to hear the stranger's gentle voice
Singing unto me in no human tones
A sweet song that the soul alone might hear :—

   O child, where wilt thou rest?—
   There on the mountain's breast,
   Where, on a crag of stone
    The eagle builds her nest?
   Or in this softer zone,
    Where sweet, warm winds o' the west
   Through flowery bowers are blown?
    O brightest soul and best,
    Where wilt thou rest?

>Oh, why make longer flight,
>Flying from morn to night?
>Oh, wherefore wander away,
>   When thou wilt find it best,
>To fold thy wings and stay?
>   Child, in mine arms be prest,
>Soul, do not longer stray;
>   Here, on thy mother's breast,
>Canst thou not rest?

At last we rested under a green tree,
Close to the gentle bubbling of a brook
Wherein a lamb, with shadow in the pool
Wool-white and soft, was drinking quietly—
And smiling down, I said, 'A heavenly place!
The very air beyond Christopolis
Is sweeten'd with the holy City's breath.'
Then, turning to the stranger, I exclaim'd—
'Unhappy one! fain would I know thy name,
Thy nurture, and thy history more at length.
Tell me—perchance I may persuade thee then
To pass unto the blessèd Gate with me,
And ask forgiveness of its Lord and King.'

I ceased in wonder; for the other lay
Smiling like one in a deep trance, his face
Looking to heaven through the tremulous boughs,

His eyes grown soft with dew of deepest joy,
The light of Nature flowing on his frame
Bright and baptismal. 'Friend,' the musical voice
Answer'd, now thrilling like the skylark's song,
'The law which made me and the law I keep
Absolve me, and my sins are all forgiven.
I take them not to market in the town,
I put no price upon them, vaunt them not;
I bring them hither, under a green tree,
And the sun drinks them, and my soul is shriven.
Oh, blest were men if to the quiet heart
Of their great Mother they crept oftener:
Her arms are ever open, her great hope
As inexhaustible as the sweet milk
With which she feeds innumerable young;
And pillow'd here, upon her own bright breast,
Safe through all issues I can pity those
Who waste their substance in Christopolis.'

Amazed I cried, 'If I conceive thee right,
Wiser is he who lieth in a dream,
Idly revolting, drowsy, indolent,
Than he who like his fellows fareth on?
These fields are sweet—'tis bright and golden
    weather—
But when the cold rain cometh, and the snow,

Where wilt thou house?'
                    Smiling, he answer'd me:
'Where do the raven and the wood-dove house,
And all things through all seasons? He who made
Will evermore preserve me. Knowest thou
Whose feet trod o'er these fields to make them
         fair,
Whose soft hand hung those boughs with orient gold,
Whose finger mark'd the curves of yonder brook,
Setting it loose and teaching it to flow
Like a thing living, singing on for ever?—
The Kings of Kings!'
                    'Dost thou believe on Him?—
Come, then, where He awaits thee, in the walls
His chosen have uprear'd.'
                    'I tell thee, friend,'
Answer'd the gentle dreamer darkening,
'I know that City to the topmost spire,
And though a thousand kings keep wassail there
He dwelleth not among them. Men uprear'd
That City, calling it Christopolis,
And marvellously it hath grown and thriven.
But, long ere that or any City arose,
These and a million greener fields and woods
Were fashion'd; how, I know not, but 'twas done;
And in the dead of night, miraculously,

Before man was, the golden wonder grew.
Then Man was made—a bright and naked thing
That in the sunshine like an antelope
Leapt in the swiftness of his liberty;
And as the small birds choose their mates, he chose
A creature bright and naked like himself,
And in the greenwood boughs they made their nest
And rear'd their callow young, singing for joy.
This was man's golden age; his race increased,
Drank the free sunshine, hunger'd, and were fed,
And knew not superstition or disease.
With the first building of a human house
Against the innocent air and the sweet rain,
The age of fire began, which hath indeed
Not yet fulfill'd its fierce and fatal course.
For on the hearth they kindled cruel flame,
And out of flame have sprung by slow degrees,
Self-multiplying, self-engendering,
The fiery scorpions of unholy arts
Innumerable that afflict mankind.
And priests at last arose, and out of fire
They fashion'd the Creator and Avenger
Who with a thousand names pollutes the earth;
Who built up yonder City; who usurps
The name and privilege of deity;
Who slew the Adam in humanity

And crucified the Christ; whose thousand spires
Shoot yonder up like forks of primal flame
Staining the blue sky and the snow-white cloud;
Who makes that evil which was fashion'd good,
And blurs the crystal of Eternity.'

Then did I think, ' He raves !' but gently said,
' These things thou say'st are hard to understand.'

' Tread through the mazes of Christopolis,
And thou shalt understand them, marvelling
What brought thee hither on so fond a quest;'
And rising, with his eyes in anger fix'd
On the great dazzle of the far-off domes,
Across the gentle fields he wander'd on.
But, following him, I whisper'd in his ear :
' Much hast thou told me, but thou hast not told
That which I ask'd—thy name and history ?'

' My name is Eglantine,' the man replied ;
He added, ' Brief is my soul's history :
A crying out for light that hath not shone,
A sowing of sweet seeds that will not spring,
A prayer, a tumult, and an ecstasy.
But come ! I see thy foolish soul is bent
Still to fare onward to Christopolis ?

Come, then, and see, as I have seen, the Tomb
Paven with pain and crownèd with a Cross.'

Through fields with orchids sprinkled, under banks
Trellis'd with honeysuckle and sweet-briar,
By sweetly flowing runlets, now we pass'd,
And with mine eager eyes fix'd still like stars
Upon the far-off Gate, I noted not
That as we went the fields and the green ways
Grew wanner and the waving grass less green,
Until we came upon that open waste
Which lieth all around the mighty City,
And through the heart of which the highway winds
Up to the western walls.
                      Upon a tract
Of lonely stone doth stand Christopolis,
And all around for leagues the rocks and sands
Stretch bleak and bare; and not a bird thereon
Flieth, save kite and crow; and here and there,
At intervals, black Crosses point the path,
And whitely strewn at every Cross's feet
There bleach the bones of pilgrims who have died.

But if the waste was bare around about
What did I heed, since now at every step
I saw the City growing fairer far;

The spires and arches all innumerable
Flashing their flame at heaven; a million roofs
Of gold and silver mirroring the skies;
Windows of pearl in sunlight glistening
Prismatic; temples and cathedrals blent
In one large lustre of delight and dream;
And presently there came a solemn sound
Of many organs playing, of deep voices
Uplifted in a strange celestial hymn,
So that the City stirr'd like one great heart
In solemn throbs of happiness and praise.

BOOK IV.

WITHIN CHRISTOPOLIS.

AGAIN we trod the highway, midst the crowd,
Close to the western walls. At last we stood
Close to the very Gate.

     The Gate was broad
For those who rode a-horse or swiftly drave
Their golden chariots through, but narrow indeed
The pathways were for those who fared a-foot;
And on the walls stood priests, from head to heel
Enswath'd in scarlet and in gold, and bearing
Crosses of silver in their outstretch'd hands;
Who cried, ' Be welcome, ye who enter in!'
But now I shrank afraid, for o'er the Gate
A naked Form with piercèd hands and feet,
Carven colossal in red agate stone,
Hung awful, with a crown upon His head.

But soon the surge of strugglers sent us on
Along the narrow path and past the priests,

Who saw us not, for all their eyes were fix'd
Upon a lion-headed Conqueror,
Who, with his moaning captives in his train
And bloody warriors round him, enter'd in.
But as the stranger in his Eastern raiment
Was passing, one cried, 'Stay!' and named his name:
Another, 'Scourge him back!' but Eglantine
Sped on, and, running, joined me presently;
While all the priests forgot him, welcoming
With smiles a lean and senile King who came
Barefoot, in sackcloth, with a sickly smile
Of false humility. Behind walk'd slaves,
Carrying his crown and sceptre.
                              Hast thou stood
Within some vast cathedral's organ-loft
While the great organ throbs, the stone walls stir,
The thunder of the deep ecstatic bass
Trembles like earthquake underfoot, the flame
Of the bright silvern flutes shoots heavenward,
And music like a darkness and a flame
Gathers and kindles, wrapping in its cloud
The great cathedral to its upmost spire?
Ev'n so, but more immeasurably strange,
Throbb'd solemn music through Christopolis;
And all my soul grew sick with rapturous awe

As slowly to the sound I moved along,
Amid the shining temples, silver shrines,
Solemn cathedrals, shadowy cloister walls,
Under the golden roofs, beneath the spires
With fiery fingers pointing up at Heaven.
Far overhead, from glittering dome to dome,
Flew doves, so high in air they seem'd as small
As wingèd butterflies, and mid the courts
Paven with bright mosaic and with pearl,
Walk'd, wrapt in saintly robes of amethyst,
Processions of the holy, singing psalms,
While smoke of incense swung in censers bright
Blew round them, rosy as a sunset cloud.

From a great temple's open door there came
Wafts of rich perfume, and we enter'd in
To music of its own deep organ-heart;
And all within was glorious, brightly hung
With pictures fairer than a poet's dream:
The King as infant in his golden hair,
Madonna mother smiling through her tears,
With forms and faces most ineffable
Of pale dead saints crownèd with aureoles.
But as the ruby brightens to the core
The temple to its inmost kindled on,
And there, around a fiery flashing shrine, .

Grave priests in white and crimson kindled flame
And chaunted, moving slowly to and fro.
Over their heads a naked bleeding Christ,
Like that above the City's mighty Gate,
Hung painted with a wan and wistful smile.

From door to door we pass'd, from shrine to shrine,
Dazzled with sight and sound; my happy eyes
So feeding on each wonder of the way
That they perceived not at each temple's porch
Black heaps of crouching men and women, clad
In rags, who clutch'd me as I enter'd in.
At last one held me by the robe, and cried
'For Christ's sake, stay!' and, turning, I perceived
A piteous skeleton that lived and spake;
Through his black sockets, like a lamp within,
His soul burnt with a faint and feverish fire.
'What thing art thou?' I cried.
                                And to my cry
No answer came but these despairing words,
'Bread! Give me bread!'
                          When, like a house of cards,
The wretch sank down again amid his rags,
Swooning.
               Then I perceived that round about
Were scatter'd many thousand such as he;

Face downward, lying on the paven ways,
Crawling like things unclean.
                              Aghast I stood,
As if the fiery levin at my feet
Had fallen and flamed; and pausing thus I saw
Stealing before me to a choral strain
A choir of women pale in black array'd;
And many look'd upon me vacantly
With rayless eyes whence the sweet light had fled;
But one white wanton tall and golden-hair'd
Laugh'd low and laughing made a sign obscene.
I started back as from a blow.
                              'Behold!'
Low spake the gentle eremite my guide,
'Behold the City of Christopolis.
Over these streets when they were desert sands
The gentle Founder of the City walk'd
Barefooted, with a beggar's staff and scrip,
Saying, "Abandon pride and follow me!"
I tell thee, friend, were that pale Paraclete
To tread these shining streets this very hour
He would not find a spot to rest His head!
Above His ashes they have built their pride
Higher than Nineveh or Babylon;
And mighty craftsmen from a hundred lands
Have flock'd to raise these temples for His tomb.

Behold it! beautiful, yet still a tomb!
For Him, and for a million such as He!
'Arise, ye dead!'
 He stood erect and cried,
Waving wild hands above him, and his cry
Seem'd answer'd. From the darken'd temple-doors,
From secret byways and from sunless lanes,
As if uprising from the very earth,
Innumerable wretches wrapt in rags,
Famish'd for food, and crippled by disease,
Crawl'd out into the sun!   Like one that sees
Legions of spectres round his midnight bed,
I stood, appall'd and pale;—around my path
They swarm'd like locusts: many knelt and wail'd,
Crying for alms; but others cross'd themselves,
Smiling; and some, in ghastly merriment,
Hooted, and moan'd, or utter'd woeful hymns.
'It is a festival,' said Eglantine,
'That brings these things unclean from out their
 holes—
A Hunt of Kings, with bloody Priests for hounds,
Will chase a heretic across the town.'

Even as he spake there gather'd on my sense
A sullen murmur as of mighty crowds;
And soon, as riseth up the ocean-tide

Filling each creek and cavern with its waves,
The streets, the open places, and the squares,
Were throng'd with living souls. Around my form
They wash'd like waters, ever lifting me,
Surging me hither and thither eagerly;
And on the roofs, and on the belfry-towers,
And in the stainèd windows of the shrines,
They throng'd—a foam of faces flashing white
Above me, hungry for the coming show.
But Priests with scourges stood along the road
Beating the people back; and Priests on high
Rang bells, and sang; and Priests amid the crowd
Mingled as thick as blood-red poppies blowing
Amid the yellow grain in harvest fields.

At last a cry arose, ' They come! They come!'

Now far away along the mighty street
The pageant came: first, fleeter than the pard,
The hunted man, not naked like that other
Who found the temple of Iconoclast,
But like a priest in crimson raimented
And on his heaving breast a snow-white Cross—
Tall was he, sinewy as a mountain deer,
And back behind him blew his reverend hair,
And white his face was, set in agony,

With eyes that look'd behind him fearfully.
Swift thro' the throng pass'd, and all the crowd
Shriek'd out in hate, even wretches in their rags
Calling a curse upon him.   Close behind
Lagg'd his pursuers :—first, the panting pack
With blood-shot eyes and teeth prepared to tear,
So hideous in their lost humanity
They seem'd not mortal men but hounds indeed ;
And after them, with gleaming swords and
 spears,
Gallop'd on foaming steeds the eager Kings,
Each King a hideous dwarf with robe and crown,
With Queens among them whose large lustful eyes
Hunger'd for blood.   Then, as I stood and gazed,
I saw a thing so glorious that it seem'd
A wondrous rainbow fallen in the street ;
For in the centre of the company,
Upraised supreme beneath a panoply,
Sat one so old and dumb at first he seem'd
A heathen idol from the banks of Ind—
White was his hair as snow, infirm his frame
Pillow'd upon a bed of purple dye,
And looking on him one might deem him dead,
Save for the senile glimmer in the eyes
That ever look'd about them vacantly—

Around him broke a blood-red surge of Priests
Wildly uplifting and upbearing him,
And ever chaunting, as they led him on,
'O holy! holy!'
                        'Whose is yonder shape?'
I questioned; and the gentle voice spake low:—
'He hath a hundred names;—in ancient times,
With mad idolatry, they called him Baal;
Usurper and inheritor is he
Of Him who built the City long ago.'

Past swept the train, that Idol in its midst,
The vast crowd like a torrent following,—
But suddenly the hunters paused, the tide
Of life wash'd back from some dark barrier,
And high on air there rose a bitter cry
That he they hunted had escaped their wrath
And taken refuge deep in sanctuary.

Then forward journeying by slow degrees,
We twain, I, Ishmael, and my gentle guide,
Came to a mighty square girt round about
With towers and temples multitudinous;
And at the centre of the square there stood,
Close-shut, a brazen Gate encalender'd
With awful shapes and legends of the Cross;

And baffled at this Gate like angry waves,
The Kings, the Queens, and many thousand Priests,
Stood clamouring in the sunlight, angrily.
'What meaneth this?' I whisper'd—'Whither now
Hath fled the man?'—and Eglantine replied,
'I did not tell thee what is simple sooth—
This gracious City of Christopolis,
One as it seemeth, indivisible,
A corporal City shining in the sun,
Is twain in soul and substance, Cities twain
Divided by that brazen Gate thou seest;
And citizens who dwell beyond that gate
Approve not yonder Idol or his slaves,
Nor love so deep the pomp of masonry,
Old custom, or the habit of the Priest.
Nay, what is holy sooth beyond the Gate
Within this square may be foul blasphemy!
He gain'd the Gate—they open'd;—pray to God
That he may *there* find peace!'

       Loudly he spake,
In tones of one accustom'd to propound,
And many round him listen'd to his words,
Whispering among each other. As he ceased
There came up panting one of those red hounds
Fixing a fever'd eye upon his face,

And crying, 'Have I found thee lingering here?—
A snake! A snake!—we thrust him forth before,
But here he crawls again!'—and suddenly
He thrust his hand out seizing Eglantine,
And beckon'd to his comrades clustering round
Like hungry wolves that dog the wounded deer.
'Back!—touch me not!' he cried, and shook him off.
But round him flocking rude and ravenous
They cried, 'To judgment!'—and before he wist
They dragg'd him to that circle of pale Kings
Baffled and clamorous for a victim, now
The hunted had escaped beyond the Gate;
And in the midst sat wan and woe begone
That hoary human Idol on its throne,
Clad head to foot in crimson and in gold,
Yet pitiful, with its poor witless eyes
And threads of hoary hair.

      'A snake! a snake!'
All shrieked, upleaping and uplifting him.
But calmer, colder than the evening star
He shone amongst them, shaking them away.
'Come to thy Judge!' they cried—and with a smile
He answer'd, 'Peace!—where is he? I will come
Before him willingly!'—A hundred hands
Uppointing at the Idol, cried, 'Behold!'
But folding his thin arms across his breast,

And fixing on the senile face a gaze
Of utter pity and more piteous scorn :
'*That!*—God have mercy on the Judge and judged
If that poor worm be mine!'
                            'A heretic!'
Clamoured a thousand throats; those hundred Kings
Prick'd up their ears and listen'd eagerly;
The red hounds leapt and panted scenting prey—
The pale Queens smiled, prepared for cruel sport—
While that wan Idol, tottering as he stirr'd,
Roll'd hollow eyeballs at the empty air
And shook a sceptre in his palsied hands.
Then, stepping forward from the crimson ranks,
While all the crowd was hush'd to hear him speak,
Stood one as gaunt as any skeleton
Bearing a sable cross in his right hand;
Who, fixing chilly eyes on Eglantine,
Thus question'd, ' Hear'st thou, man!—Dost thou deny
Our master's right to judge thee?'

EGLANTINE.
                            I deny
That Image, yet denying pity him
For his weak age and poor humanity.

INQUISITOR.

Dost thou deny the heir elect o' the King?
Now shall I catch thee tripping, for perchance
Thou dost deny the Lord our King Himself?

EGLANTINE.

Instruct me further, for I know not yet,
Since Kings are many, of what King ye speak?

INQUISITOR.

Of Him who was from all Eternity,
Who clothed Himself in likeness of a man,
Who died, with His red blood upbuilt the City
And sealed it with His name, Christopolis.

EGLANTINE.

I have not seen Him, and I know Him not;
But if a god be judged like man by works,
And thy God fashion'd this Christopolis,
I do deny Him, and reject Him too,
As much as I reject that Spectre there.

Rose from the throats of all that multitude
A shriek of horror and of cruelty,

The red hounds wail'd, the Kings drew out their
    swords,
While I did close mine eyes in agony
Fearing to see that gentle brother slain.
But still serene as any star his face
Smiled and made calm the tempest once again,
While with uplifted hand and quivering lips,
Pallid with rage, the Inquisitor spake on.

Inquisitor.

Now I perceive thee atheist as thou art—
Dost thou believe in any King that is?

Eglantine.

I know not. What is he thou callest King?

Inquisitor.

The Maker of the heavens and the earth,
Dumb monsters and the seeing soul of man:
The first strange Force, the first and last Supreme,
Shaper of all things, and Artificer.

Eglantine.

Some things are evil—if He fashion'd evil,
And leaves it evil, then I know Him not.

INQUISITOR.

If He made evil (and *thou*, too, art evil)
To be a testimony unto good,
Answer me straight—dost thou believe on Him?

EGLANTINE.

Nay, give me breath, and I will answer thee
According to the measure of my seeing.
Thou questionest if I believe i' the King?
I do believe in Law and Light and Love,
If these be He, I do believe in Him;
And in mine Elder Brother I believe
Because He suffer'd and His voice is sweet,
But though He was the fairest of us all,
A mortal like myself He lived and died;
And when I wander out in yonder fields,
Under the opening arch of yonder heaven,
Beyond the fatal shadows of these Kings,
Beyónd the City's dark idolatries,
A Spirit uplifts my hair, anoints mine eyes,
Sweetens my sight, and, if this Spirit be He,
With all my heart I do believe in Him;
And when in peace I close mine eyes and watch
The calm reflection of all shining things

Mirror'd within me as within a brook,
And feel the scatter'd images of life,
Like broken shadows in a pool, unite
To lineaments most mystic and divine,
I do believe, I verily believe,
For God is with me, and the face of God
Looks from the secret places of my soul.
Thus much I know, and knowing question not;
But more than this I cannot comprehend.
The Everlasting and Imperishable
Eludes me, as the sight of the sweet stars
That shine uncomprehended yet serene;
For nightly, silently, their eyes unclose,
And whoso sees their light, and gazes on it
Till wonder turns to rapture, seemeth ever,
Like one that reads all secrets in Love's eyes,
Swooning upon the verge of certainty—
Another look, another flash, it seems
And all God's mystery will be reveal'd,
But very silently they close again,
Shutting their secret 'neath their silvern lids,
And looking inward with a million orbs
On the Unfathomable far within
Their spheres, as is the soul within the soul.
God is *their* secret;—but I turn to Earth,
My Mother, and in her dark fond face I gaze,

Still questioning until at last I find
Her secret, and its sweetest name is Love:
And this one word she murmurs secretly
Into the ears of birds and beasts and men;
And sometimes, listening to her, as she lies
Twining her lilies in her hair, and watching
Her blind eyes as they glimmer up to heaven,
I dream this word she whispers to herself
Is yet another mystic name of God.

More would his lips have spoken, but the shriek
Of 'Atheist! Atheist!' drown'd his gentle
    voice—
And as around some gentle boat at sea
Riseth a sudden storm of sharp-tooth'd waves,
So rose that company of Priests and Kings;
And as a boat is wash'd and whirl'd and
    driven
'Mid angry breakers, from beyond my sight
The dreamer's fair frail form was borne away,—
Yet ever and anon I saw his face
Arise seraphic 'mid the blood-red sea,
Undaunted, undespairing, and as yet
Unharm'd! The tumult rose. Kings, Priests,
    and Slaves,
Were mix'd confusedly, as to and fro

The great crowd eddied; and I sought in vain
To reach the dreamer's side and speak with him;
But when I call'd his name despairingly,
A hundred hands were lifted on myself,
A hundred fingers trembled at my throat,
And voices shriek'd, 'Another—death to him!'
Back was I fiercely driven, step by step,
And more than once I stagger'd to my knees,
My raiment rent, my body bruised and beaten,
My spirit like a lamp swung in a storm
Blurr'd, darken'd, shedding only straggling beams
Of feeble sense. 'Almighty King,' I moan'd,
'Is *this* thy City?'
     As I spake the words
I stagger'd to that mighty brazen Gate,
And looking up I saw enwrought thereon
These words—'Knock here if thou wouldst
  enter in.'
I turn'd once more, and saw the people's faces
Flashing in fury round me—swords and staves
Uplifted—arms outstretching for my throat:
Sick with that sight, I knock'd, and ere I knew
The Gate swung open—hands outreaching grasp'd
My fainting form and dragg'd me swiftly in;—
And as a bark out of an angry sea
Ploughs round a promontory into calm,

Then slips on silent where all winds are dead
Into a quiet haven in the bay,
I found myself beyond the brazen Gate,
Panting, unharm'd, while from my awe-struck ears,
Miraculously, instantaneously,
The murmur of that tumult died away.

BOOK V.
WITHIN THE GATE.

BREATHLESS, a space I paused, breathless and blind,
Then slowly as a wight that wakes from sleep
Gazed round me ; and behold I found myself
Within a great quadrangle dark and still,
Uplooking on the other side o' the Gate
Whereon was written in a fiery scroll :
' No path—beware the many-headed Beast !'
And gather'd round me as I shuddering stood
I saw a group of silent men in black,
Sad-featured, holding each an open book.
' Where am I now ?' I murmur'd vacantly,
One of those strangers with a pensive smile
Answer'd, ' In safety, friend ! within this Gate
They cannot harm thee. Welcome, weary one,
To the blest shelter of Christopolis.'

Whereat I cried : ' Accursèd be the name,
Which lured me from blue heaven and the sweet
          fields !

For he was wise who warn'd me ere I came,
And now I know the City as it is,
Not holy like the City of my dream,
But evil, cruel, dreary, and defiled.'
'Blaspheme not,' said that other; 'yet in sooth
We pardon thee thy rash and ribald speech,
For thou hast seen the City's evil side.
Beyond that Gate there reigneth Antichrist
In likeness of the foul and loathsome Beast,
But here, in verity, thy storm-toss'd heart
May rest in peace.'
      And now, within my dream,
Methought I wander'd on with those grave men,
And listen'd, hoping, yet in half despair,
To their soft speech. Less golden and less bright
The City seem'd upon its thither side,
For everywhere upon the sunless streets
Dark temples and black-arch'd cathedrals cast
A solemn shadow, and the light within
Was sadder-temper'd and more soul-subduing,
And solemner the mighty music seem'd
That sigh'd through every crevice like a sea.
Yet overhead the same bright fingers shot
Their flames at heaven, and the white doves flew,
And patient look'd the azure light of heaven
Fretted by domes and arches numberless

Yet brooding most serene.
                       But now my soul
Did scent for evil with a keener sense,
And that fair-seeming show of sight and sound
O'ercame me not, but ever I look'd abroad
In sorrow and mistrust; and soon indeed
My search was answer'd; for I saw again,
Low-lying near the black cathedral doors,
Forms of the wretched writhing in their rags,
And peering in through the wide-open doors
I saw the shapes of Kings bright-raimented
Who knelt at prayer. Then turning unto those
Who led me, bitterly I smiled and said:
'Meseems ye have kept your carrion and your
    Kings,
As they have yonder—Plainly I perceive
That still I walk within Christopolis!'

One answer'd: 'God forbid that we should miss
Their company who are divinely crown'd;
And for the poor, hath not the King of Kings
Enjoin'd upon His servants to have these
For ever with them?'

                      'Tell me roundly then,
What must he do who would within this Gate

Be deem'd a good and lawful citizen?
Must he bow down to Idols such as those
They carry yonder? Must he quake at Priests?
And, if he must be judged, who judgeth him?'

'Good man, thou knowest little of this place
If thou dost dream that we who dwell herein
Will kneel to any Idol or accept
The will of perishable Priests or Kings.
Upon that score we parted first with those
Our neighbours, choosing here to dwell apart.
Be one of us, and surely thou shalt bow
Neither to Idol nor to mortal man,
Nor shalt thou quake at any mortal judge;
Nay, shouldst thou need a judge that judge shall be
Thine own good conscience and the City's law.'

Then did I brighten, somewhat comforted,
Yet nothing now could waken in my soul
That old first faith wherewith I saw from far
The flashing of the City's thousand spires—
And to myself I said: 'A bootless dream,
A dreary City and a bootless dream,
If this be all!' So with a heavy heart
I look'd upon the temples and the shrines,

And heard the solemn music welling forth,
And saw the quiet folk that came and went,
Silent and quick, like bees that throng i' the hive.

Now, as I wander'd musing, I beheld
One who sat singing at a temple door,
His face illumined, turning soft with tears
Upward and sunward; and the song he sang
Was low and hush'd as is the nightingale's
Just as the dusky curtain of a cloud
Is drawn across the bright brow of the moon;
And, lo! I listen'd, for it seem'd the song
Came from the deep heart of mine own despair,
And tears were in mine eyes before it ceased.

>Come again, come back to me,
>   White-wing'd throng of childish Hours,
>Lead me on from lea to lea,
>   Ankle-deep in meadow-flowers;
>Set a lily in my hand,
>   Weave wild pansies in my hair,
>Through a green and golden land
>   Lead me on with fancies fair.
>White-wing'd Spirits, come again,—
>   Heal my pain!
>Through the shadows of the rain
>   Come again!

Come again, and by me sit
 As you sat that summer day,
Seeing through the mists of heat
 This great City far away.
Golden glow'd its magic fires
 Far across the valleys green,
Heavenward flash'd its thousand spires,
 Silent, trembling, faintly seen.
Show thy visions once again,
  White-wing'd train!
With the dream I dream'd in vain,
  Come again!

Come again, and lead me back
 To the fields and meadows sweet,
Softly, by the self-same track
 Follow'd by my coming feet;
From the City's gates set free,
 Backward to the gates of morn—
Every backward step will be
 Brighter, fairer, less forlorn.
Lead me! let me reach again
  Wood and lane—
Lead me to your green domain
  Once again.

Come again!—but, O sweet Hours!
 If ye come *not* ere I die,
Find me dead, with bands of flowers
 Lift me up from where I lie,

> Take me to the woodland place
>   Where I linger'd long ago,
> Set soft kisses on my face,
>   Singing, as ye lay me low—
> Let me slumber there again,
>   Far from pain—
> Waking up with weary brain,
>   Ne'er again!

Methought that as that song of sad despair
Rose like a murmuring fountain, all the place
Darken'd as when the sun is lost in clouds;
And from the temples, from the clustering dwellings,
There rose in answer one great wail of pain,
Which breaking like a wave was spent in tears;
And, lo! mine own tears fell, for I remember'd
The meadows where I wander'd when a child,
The baptism of my love new born in joy
And looking on a sun-illumined world.
Then one of those grave dwellers in the City,
Turning upon me dark and ominous eyes,
Said, ''Tis the music which the Snake did
        weave
To mock the first of man when he had fallen—
Self-pity is the mournful slave of sin;
Do thou beware in time!' whereon I cried,
'A light is lost that never will return:

What canst thou give me now to heal the heart
Made desolate as dust?'

'Pray!'

'I have pray'd!'

'Wait!'

'I have waited!'

'If thy spirit fail,
Turn to the living wonder of the Word!'

Then I perceived that he with whom I spake
Held in his hand an open Book like that
I bare within my breast; and gazing round
I saw that every shape within those streets
Did hold a Book wide open as he walk'd,
Reading aloud and muttering to himself
Prayer, parable, and psalm. Wherefore I cried,
'I know that comfort; it was given for bread,
But turn'd to bitterest wormwood long ago!'
Then ere I knew it I was circled round
With faces terrible and white as death,
And one, a hoary wight with eyes of fire,
Shriek'd, 'Strike him down, O thunderbolt of
God!

He doth deny Thine everlasting Word!'
But one, more gentle, interposing, said:
'Silence, and list unto him. Pilgrim, speak;
Dost thou deny God's message unto men?'

The Pilgrim.

Nay, I deny it not, but I have heard
That message, and I find no comfort there.

Stranger.

No comfort in the justice of the Lord?
No succour in the mercy of the Son?

The Pilgrim.

Sad is that justice, woeful is the mercy,
Most dark the testimony of the Book;
But yonder, out beyond the City's wall,
The sun shines golden, and the earth is merry,
And only here the grievous shadow lies.

Stranger.

The shadow of thy sin, which sin is death.
Answer again: Believest thou the Book?

THE PILGRIM.
As I believe in thunders and in storm.

STRANGER.
Dost thou reject all other testimonies,
Holding this only as the voice of God?

THE PILGRIM.
Nay, for I hear it as the voice of men.

STRANGER.
Dost thou believe these wonders written down?

THE PILGRIM.
Nay, for among them many are most sad,
Some are incredible, and all most strange.

STRANGER.
Rejectest thou the Book's own testimony,
That all these mysteries are truths divine?

THE PILGRIM.
No book can testify unto itself;
Nor is that Book a living voice at all!

STRANGER.

These tokens testify to Word and Book:
The lights of Heaven and Hell; the voice of God
Heard in the beating of the human heart;
Christ's burial; last, His rising from the grave.
Denyest thou these?

THE PILGRIM.

    Heaven have I fail'd to find;
Hell have I found on earth, and in thy City;
The voice of mine own soul rejects the voice
I once did hear in my affrighted heart;
I do believe Christ's burial, but, alas!
Why is the gentle promise unfulfill'd?
Why doth the world's pale Martyr rest unrisen?

STRANGER.

In spirit He hath risen—lo, His City,
To testify His prescience and His power.

Ev'n as he spake, there pass'd along the street
A host of armèd men in black array'd,
Led on by one who rode a sable steed
And wore a helmet shapen like a crown;

These to Jehovah as they march'd did raise
A sullen hymn of praise for victory,
And some were to the ankles shod in blood,
But many as they march'd did gravely read
The open pages of the Holy Book.
'What men are these?' I ask'd, and one
    replied:
'Warriors of Christ, who walk about the world
Slaying and smiting in the blessèd Name!'

Then, laughing low in bitterness of heart,
I saw the doors and casements opening wide,
And faces thronging with a wicked joy
To welcome back the warriors of the Lord.
Moreover, as I gazed, mine eyes could mark
Dark chambers full of grave and silent men
Who sat at ebon tables counting gold,
And 'mid the golden heaps that each did pile
The open Scripture lay; and down the streets
Came men who waved their hands, and cried,
    'Repent!'
And here and there, in lonely darken'd places,
The Tree of man's invention rose and swung
With human fruitage dead and horrible;
And 'neath that Tree more woeful voices rose,
Crying, 'Repent and die! Repent and die!'

And million voices echoed back the sound,
And even those silent men who counted gold
Moan'd answer from the darkness of their dens.

Then cried I, 'He was wise who warn'd me,
    saying,
" Thy sepulchre, O bleeding Nazarene,
Is still thy sepulchre!" Thy dream was peace,
But lo, destruction, sorrow, and a sword;
Thy prayer was for the poor and meek of heart,
But lo, the golden gloom and dust of pride;
Thy creed was mercy for the worst and best,
But lo! the hideous Tree and not the Cross;
Thy light was sunshine and a shining place,
But, lo! deep dread and darkness of the Book;'
And turning to those men who follow'd me,
' The black leaves of the Book are blossomless,
And of its upas-fruit whoever eats
Bears wormwood in his heart for evermore.'

'Blasphemer!' answer'd one in night-black
    robes,
And hollow-eyed as Famine throned on graves;
' The Gospel which is wormwood in the mouth
Is honey being eaten and consumed.
Evil are mortals, evil is the world,

Evil are all things man hath written down ;
But this one thing is absolutely good :
Read it, and live ; cast it away, and die.'

The Pilgrim.

I'll read no more ;—fairer to me by far
That Book I read, not understanding yet,
Upon the lonely shores where I was born.

Citizen.

What Book is that ? and written by whose hand ?

The Pilgrim.

By God's in the beginning ; on its front
He set the stars for signs, the sun for seal ;
Golden the letters, bright the shining pages,
Holy the natural gospel, of the earth ;
Blessèd tenfold the language of that Book
For ever open ; blessèd he who reads
The leaf that ever blossoms ever turn'd !

Citizen.

This Book I hold doth prove that other dust ;
Its brightness is a fleshly sin and snare.

The Pilgrim.

He made it; left it open for our seeing.

Citizen.

The shadow of the primal sin remains.
There, on the fallen rose-leaves of the world,
The snake crawls, as in Eden long ago.

Upon me, as he spake, methought there fell
A shadow like that shadow which he fear'd;
And in its midst, as in some night of storm
The crested billows flash with gleams of foam,
The faces of those sombre citizens
Glimmer'd around. Mad with mine own despair
I stood as on some dreary promontory
Looking on tempest of a sunless sea—
'Behold the Book!' I cried, while from my
    breast
I drew it forth and held it high in air;
'Here in mine bosom it hath lain for long,
Chiller than ice and heavy as a stone;
I cast it back as bread upon the waters—
Uplift it, wear it on his heart who will,
Henceforward I reject it utterly.'

So saying I threw it from me, while a shriek
Of horror rose from that black crowd of men;
And ere I knew it I was circled round
With living waters rising high in wrath
To drown and to devour and dash me down.
'Death to him! to the foul blasphemer, death!'
'Wrath to the wretch who doth reject the Word!'
'Ah, Satan, Satan!' rose the murderous cries,
While all in vain I sought to shield my head
Against a shower of ever-increasing blows;
And, lo! again, I saw the doors and casements
Were open, and wild faces looking forth,
And warriors pointed at me with their swords,
And women rushing with dishevell'd hair
Shriek'd 'Vengeance!' till meseem'd before my feet
The very pit of Hell was yawning wide,
While flame flash'd up, and smoke of fire arose,
Scorching my sense and blotting from my sight
The towers and temples of Christopolis.

But as I struggled crying out on God,
Methought that one in raiment white and fair
Strode to me through the horror of the crowd
And held me up from falling, while the cry
Grew louder, 'Cast him out beyond the Gate!
Slay him, and cast him forth!' and as a straw

Is lifted on a torrent, I was raised,
And wildly, darkly, desolately driven
I knew not whither. From the earth still rose
Darkness and fire; fire from the heavens overhead
Seem'd following: baleful fire did wrap me round
As with red raiment—but that succouring hand
Still held me, and a low voice in mine ear
Cried, 'Courage,' as I drifted dumbly on.

From street to street, from lane to lane, methought
They drove me, bruised and bleeding, till I reach'd
Another Gate, which on its hinges swinging
Open'd to let me pass, then with a clang
Did shut its soot-black jaws behind my back,
While from within I heard the sullen roar
Of those dark waters which had cast me forth.

BOOK VI.
THE CALVARIES.

AT last methought I paused, and deathly pale,
My raiment rent, my body bruised with blows,
Turn'd to my rescuer with questioning eyes
And would have spoken, but the other cried,
' Hush for a space, lest thou be overheard ! '
And not until our feet had flown full far,
Down empty byways and down darken'd lanes,
Nor till the populous walks were far behind
And we were deep in flowers and meadow-grass
Of quiet uplands, did we pause again.
And now the star of evening had arisen
Set like a sapphire in the shadowy west,
And slow crows waver'd homeward silently
With sleepy waft of wing, and all was still,
Only the far-off murmur of the City
Came like the distant thunder of a sea.

Then pausing, I upon my gentle guide
Gazed closely, and beheld a face benign,
Sweeten'd with many sorrows, sweetest eyes

Weary and weak with their own gentleness,
And lips sweet too, yet close together set
With sad resolve. Tall was the stranger's height,
His gestures noble, but his shoulders stoop'd
With some dark burthen not beheld of eyes;
And ever in his breast did creep his hand,
As if to still the tumult of his heart.
Yet, gazing on his garb, I shrank away
Sick and afraid, for lo! upon his breast
Glimmer'd the crimson Cross of those fierce Priests,
And clad he was like many in the City
In a white robe that swept unto his feet.

Darkly I cried, 'Avaunt! I know thee not!
I deem'd thee good, but thou art even as those
Who stoned me, thronging at my throat like wolves,
And sought my life;' when, with a smile as bright
As had the vesper star above his head,
'Friend, be at peace!' the gentle stranger cried,
'Nor fear mine office, by the Cross I wear!'

THE PILGRIM.

That Cross affrights my vision—pluck it off,
And I shall know thou art a man indeed.

The Stranger.

I cannot, since I am God's Priest elect;
Nay, rather in the Name of Him who bare
A Cross like this I bid thee love the sign.

The Pilgrim.

Carry thy firebrand back into the City,
I loathe it! Evil is the sign, and still
Evil its wearers wheresoe'er they walk!
Art thou a Priest? My curse upon thy head!
Avoid me!—to thy brethren—get thee gone!

Stranger.

Until thy heart is calm'd I cannot go;
Nor will I leave thee till thou hearest me.

The Pilgrim.

Thou heardst me—I proclaim'd it in the City—
False are your fables, false your boasted creeds,
Falsest of all your spirits and your lives.
There is no truth in any land at all
Ye darken, sitting by the side of Kings.

Stranger.

False Priests are false, and these thine eyes have seen.

The Pilgrim.

All Priests are false, for falsehood is their creed.

Stranger.

Phrase me my creed; if thou canst prove it false
I promise thee I will abandon it.

The Pilgrim.

How shall I name it? Which of many names
Shall fit it now? Guile, Fraud, Hypocrisy,
Blood-thirst and Blood-shed, Persecution, Pride,
Mammon—in one word sum it, Vanity.

Stranger.

Friend, thou hast miss'd the mark. Our creed is
    Love.

The Pilgrim.

I know that jargon. Spare it; for I know it.
The wolf wears wool, and calls himself a lamb.

Stranger.

Heed not our garb, or what we call ourselves—
Yea, judge not what we seem, but what we are.

The Pilgrim.

That have I done; so is my judgment proved;
For they who flaunt your banners in Love's name
Pursued me, stoned me on from street to street,
And would have slain me with their bloody hands.

Stranger.

In sooth they would, had help not intervened.
I know them well; my friend, they have stoned *me!*

The Pilgrim.

They do not spare each other, I believe;
But even as wolves, when no poor sheep is near,
They fall upon each other and devour.

Stranger.

Bitter thou art, o'er bitter, yet thy words,
Though harsh as wormwood, are in measure just,
For many Priests are false, and follow ill
The Scripture they propound to foolish flocks.
Yet mark me well; though many sought by force
To win the soul they could not win by words,
'Twas for thy soul they wrought, to save thy soul,
And insomuch, though blind, they wrought in love.

The Pilgrim.

Smiling and slaying! hungry for my life!
O Sophist! now I know thee Priest indeed.

Stranger.

Pause yet. I love their deeds no more than thou,
Yet rather would believe them doubly blind
(For blindness may be crime, but is not sin)
Than wholly base and hypocritical.
Grant that they sought thy death—through death
    they sought
To win thy spirit to eternal life!
Thou laughest, and mad mockery in thine eyes
Burneth with bloodshot beams. Resolve me now—
Dost thou deny that these same Priests are blind?

The Pilgrim.

To good, I grant thee, but for this world's goods
Who have a sense so keen; and wheresoe'er
Hath crawl'd this glittering serpent of a Church
All men may know it by these tokens twain—
Blood-marks, and next, its slimy trail of gold.
Blind are ye to the sun and moon and stars,
To good, and to the beggar at your gates;
But unto usury ye are not blind;

And into murderous eyes of Queens and Kings
Your eyes can look approval, while your mouths
Intone fond hymns to tyranny and war;
And unto raiment rich, and glittering coins,
And houses hung with crimson and with gold,
And harlots beckoning in their golden hair,
Methinks all mortals know ye are not blind!

Thus spake I in the tempest of my heart,
Now pacing up and down with fever'd steps
The twilight-shadow'd lanes beyond the City;
And now the eyes of heaven were opening,
And in dark woods hard by the nightingales
Sang softly up the slow and lingering moon.
And, hurrying my footsteps, soon I came
To where four roads did meet to make a cross,
And in the centre of the way I saw,
Dim, livid, silhouetted on the sky,
A Calvary, and thereupon a Christ
Most rudely sculptured out of crimson stone.

Thereon, methought, I halted shuddering,
Gazed, then shrank back, and cover'd up mine eyes,
When once again I noted at my side
That white-robed stranger and upon mine ear
Again the melancholy accents fell.

The Calvaries.

STRANGER.

Why shrinkest thou? Kneel down and ease thy heart.

THE PILGRIM.

Peace, peace! I will not worship wood or stone.
Who set that image here to block the way?
Nay, spare thine answer; they who wrought this thing
Are those who stoned me from Christopolis—
Thy brethren! Not the honeysuckled lanes,
The twilight-shadow'd meadows sweet with flowers,
The violet-sprinkled ways and underwoods,
Not Nature's self, not the still solitude,
Are free from this pollution dark as death,
This common horror of idolatry.

STRANGER.

Knowest thou whose shape is carven on that cross?

THE PILGRIM.

The Man Divine whom Priests of Judah slew.

STRANGER.

The Man Divine who still is hourly slain
Wherever sin is thought or wrong is done.

O brother, keep me by thy side a space,
And, looking on that symbol, hark to me.
Him did they stone, like thee and me; and yet—
Mark this, He loved them, dying for their sake.
Blame them, if they are worthy of thy blame,
Lament them, in so far as they have fallen
From the divine ideal they propound;
But still remember this, amidst thy blame—
They rear'd that Cross and set that symbol there!

THE PILGRIM.

To what avail? To darken earth's sweet ways?

STRANGER.

To hold forth hope to every living man,
To be a protestation and a power
Against their own defilement if defiled.
'Tis something to uprear a mighty truth,
Though from its eminence the weak will falls;
'Tis much to plant a beacon on the sea,
Though they who plant it lose their hold and drown.
Were each Priest evil in an evil world,
This would not prove that fair ideal false
Which for the common gaze they find and prove.
Brother, hadst thou but watch'd this place with me

By night-time, in the silence of the night!
For out of yonder City, as if ashamed,
Sad human creatures creep with hooded heads
And falling at the feet of Calvary,
Scarce conscious of each other's presence, weep
Such tears as yonder Christ deems worth a world.
And moonlight falling on their haggard faces
Hath shown the lineaments of cruel Kings
Set side by side with beggars in their rags,
And pale Queens, naked, crownless, grovelling close
To harlots with dishevell'd locks of gold,
And conscience-stricken Priests that beat their breasts
With bitterest ululations of despair.

Then did I smile, and cry, 'I doubt thee not!
What then? Next dawn thy Kings were on their thrones,
Thy Queens were crown'd, thy harlots plied their trade,
Thy beggars craved for bread and gnaw'd a stone,
Thy Priests were glorious in their gold and gems,
And all the City busy as before.
Such conscience is an owl that flies by night,
No sweet white dove that moves abroad by day;
And he who in the sunlight brazens best

Is the worst coward in night's creeping time.'
I added this, moreover, ' Since so far
Thy feet have follow'd, and since, furthermore,
I owe thee something for my weary life,
I will accost thee in a gentler mood,
Seeking thy soul's conversion even as thou
Hast sought for mine; but first I fain would know
Thy name, thine office, and thy quality.'

Whereon the other smiling, better pleased,
'My name is Merciful, the Priest of Christ,
And yonder in Christopolis I dwell
Half hated by my brethren and half fear'd,
Because I help the Pilgrims passing by
And lead them hither unto Calvary.'

THE PILGRIM.

Art thou not shamed to wear the garb they wear,
Seeing their deeds profane it terribly?

MERCIFUL.

Not so. If they fulfil their office ill,
That doth not prove the office evil too:
And wearing this white dress of sanctity
I work as one that hath authority,
And better help poor Pilgrims passing by.

The Pilgrim.

Thus far, thou workest good. Now, answer me—
Dost thou believe the fables of the Book?

Merciful.

Not in the letter, but essentially.

The Pilgrim.

Dost thou believe that still by one man's fall
We mortal men are lost and overthrown;
But yet, since God did make Himself a Man,
Attesting this by many miracles,
Through God's own Death the world may still be saved?

Merciful.

I do believe these things symbolically,
As I believe the symbol of that Cross.

The Pilgrim.

Did Jesus live and die in Galilee?
Did He work miracles and raise the dead?
Was Jesus God, and could God Jesus die?

Merciful.

I will not fall into that trap of words,
Which, grimly smiling, thou hast laid for me,
But I will answer thee as best I may,
Clearly, and with no touch of sophistry.
'Did Jesus live?' I know a sweet Word lives,
Coming like benediction on the sense
Where'er Love walks uplooking heavenward,
And since no Word is spoken without lips,
Hearing that Word I know He lived and breathed.
'Did Jesus die?' On every wayside cross,
In every market-place and solitude,
I see a symbol of a wondrous death;
And, since each symbol doth its substance prove,
How should I not believe that Jesus died?
'Did He work miracles and raise the dead?'
'Was Jesus God?'—Here is my timid sense
Lost in a silence and a mystery—
And yet I know, by every breath I breathe,
The Mighty and the Merciful are one :
The morning dew that scarcely bends the flowers
Inhaled to heaven becomes the lightning flash
That lights all heaven ere noon. 'Could Jesus die?'
If Death be Life, and Life Eternity,

VI.] *The Calvaries.* 117

If Death be but the image of a change,
Perchance even God might take the image on,
And in the splendour of His pity, die.

So spake the gentle Priest, his mild blue eye
Dewy with love for all men and for God,
But I did answer with a hollow laugh
Deep as a raven's croak, that echoed on
Through all the architraves of that blue vault
Above us bent. 'God help thee, man!' I cried;
' For thou art pleased as any yearling babe
With playthings that thou canst not understand.
Fables and symbols dazzle thy twain eyes,
And phantasies of loving sentiment
Puzzle thy reason and perplex thy will.
Wiser are they who on the tripod sit,
Intoning oracles and studying
The dry dull letter of theology,
Than they who, like to thee and such as thou,
Are drunken with its gentle images.'

'Kneel!' answer'd Merciful; 'perchance in prayer
Thine eyes may be unveil'd.'
      But I replied,
Pointing at that pale Calvary which loom'd
Dim and gigantic in the starry light,

'I will not kneel to yonder shape of stone,
If by the name of God thou callest it;
But if thou call'st it Man, Man crucified,
Man martyr'd, I will kneel, not worshipping,
But clinging to an Elder Brother's feet,
And calling on the sweetest saddest soul
That ever walk'd with bleeding limbs of clay
These solitary shades beneath the stars.
He found it not, the City that I seek,
He came and went upon His quest in vain,
And crucified upon His path by Priests
Became a portent and a piteous sign
On the great highway of man's pilgrimage;
And though the memory of His love is sweet,
The shadow of Him is cruel and full fraught
With tearfullest despairs; and wheresoe'er
We wander, we are haunted out of hope
By this pale Martyr with His heavenly eyes,
Born brightest and loved least of all the sons
Of God the Father! Could I 'scape the sight
Methinks that I could fare along in peace!'

'Never,' cried Merciful, 'where'er thou fliest,
Wilt thou escape it? Search where'er thou
    wilt,
Follow what path thou choosest, soon or late

With that red Cross thou wilt come face to face
When least thou dreamest.   On the desert sands,
On the sad shores of the sea, upon the scroll
Of the star-printed heavens, on every flower
That blossoms, on each thing that flies or creeps
'Tis made—the sign is made, the Cross is
    made—
That cipher which whoever reads can read
The riddle of the worlds.'
                      So saying, he fell
Low kneeling at the foot of Calvary,
And praying aloud; and overhead indeed
The awful sacrificial lineaments
Seem'd soften'd in the moonlight, looking down
As if they smiled.   Darkly I turn'd away
Heartsick, first wafting to that sculptured form
One look of love and pity.
                        Silently,
In meditation deep as my despair,
I follow'd the dark road I knew not whither,
As desolate as Io wandering;
And like another Argus following,
Blue heaven with all its myriad eyes on mine
Brooded; and wayside scents of honeysuckle
Came to my nostrils from the darken'd fields,
And glowworms glimmer'd through the dewy grass,

And all was sweet and still; but evermore,
At intervals, on either side I saw
New Calvaries upon the lonely road
And sculptured Christs outstretching stony arms.

BOOK VII.
THE WAYSIDE INN.

NOW as I walk'd I mused . . .
            'The Priest spake well:
The Cross is everywhere, and read aright
Is Nature's riddle; well, I read it thus—
Silent progressions to new powers of pain
Through cruel æons of blood-sacrifice.
For life is based upon the law of death,
And death is surely evil; wherefore, then,
All life seems evil. To each thing that lives
Is given, without a choice, this destiny—
To be a slayer or a sufferer,
A tyrant or a martyr; to be weak
Or cruel; to range Nature like a hawk,
Or fall in cruel talons like a dove;
And of these twain, where both are evil things,
That Cross decrees that martyrdom is best.
What then? Shall I praise God for martyrdom?
Nay!—I can drink the poison cup and die,
But bitter is the blessing I would call
On Him who mix'd it with His fatal Hand.'

The path I follow'd now was dark as death,
And overhead the ever-gathering clouds
Were charged with rain; the piteous stars were
    gone,
Blown out like tapers in a mighty wind
That wheel'd in maddening circles round the moon;
And deeper into the dark vaporous void
The moon did burn her way till she was hid
And nothing but the cloudy night remain'd.
Then the great wind descended, and, it seem'd,
In answer to it every wayside Christ
Stretch'd arms and shriek'd. Suddenly, with a groan,
The vials of the storm were open'd!
                                    Then
The rain fell, and the waters of the rain
Stream'd like a torrent; and across the shafts
Sheet-lightning glimmer'd ghastly, while afar
The storm-vex'd breakers of Eternity
Thunder'd.
            In that great darkness of the storm
Wildly I fled, and, lo! my pilgrim's robes,
Drench'd with the raindrops, like damp cerements
    clung
Around my weary limbs; and whither I went
I knew not, but as one within a maze
Drave hither and thither, with my lifted arms

Shielding my face against the stinging lash
Of rains and winds. Methought my hour was come,
For oft upon the soaking earth I fell,
Moaning aloud; yet ever again I rose
And struggled on; even so amid a sea
Of dark and dreadful waters strikes and strives
Some swimmer, half unconscious that he swims,
Yet with the dim brute habit of the sense
Fighting for life he knows not why or how,
Nor whither on the mighty billows' breast
His form is roll'd!
    But ever and anon
When, like a lanthorn dim and rain-beaten
That flasheth sometimes to a feeble flame,
My dark mind into memory was illumed,
I thought, ' Despair! I cannot last the night!
Ah, would that I had stay'd with that pale Priest,
Seeking for comfort where he findeth it.
Yea, better his half-hearted company
Than to be drifting in the tempest here,
Alone, despairing, haunted, woe-begone.
He cannot hear me. Shall I call on Christ,
His Master?—Christ! Adonai!—He is dumb,
Dumb in His silent sculptured agony—
Dead! dead!'
    I would have fallen with a shriek,

But suddenly across my aching eyes
There shot a bloodshot light as of some fire
Amid the waste. I stood, and strain'd my gaze
Into the darkness. Steady as a star
The glimmer grew, shining from far away
With slant moist beams on the black walls of rain.

Lured by the lonely ray I struggled on,
Faint, stumbling, soaking, panting, overpower'd,
But brighter as I went the glimmer grew,
And soon I saw it from the casement came
Of a dark dwelling on the weary waste.
Forlorn the dwelling stood, and on its roof
The rain smote with a cheerless leaden sound,
And in the front of it, on creaking chains,
There swung a sign. Then did my heart upleap,
Rejoicing once again in hope to feel
The touch of human hands, to hear the sound
Of human voices; and I cried aloud,
'Thank God at least for this lone hostelry,
But for its friendly help I should have died.'

So saying, I knock'd, and as I knock'd I heard,
Faint, far within, a sound of revelry
From distant rooms; but still the cruel rain
Smote on me, and above my head the sign

Moan'd like a corse in chains. I knock'd again
More clamorously, striking with my staff—
And soon I heard the shuffling of slow feet
Approaching. Hearing this, I knock'd the more,
And then, with creak and groan of locks and keys,
The door swung open, and before mine eyes
Loom'd a great lobby in the midst of which
A marble-featured serving-maiden stood,
Sleepy, half yawning, holding in her hand
A dismal light. Bloodless her cheeks and cold,
Her hair a golden white, her eyes dead blue,
Her stature tall, and thin her shrunken limbs
And chilly hands. 'Welcome!' she murmur'd low,
Not marking me she welcomed but with eyes
All vacant staring out into the night.
'Who keeps this house?' I question'd, rushing in,
And as she closed and lock'd the oaken door
The maiden answer'd with a far-off look,
Like one that speaks with ghosts, ' My master, sir,
Host Moth ; and we are full of company
This night, and all the seasons of the year.'

Even then, along the lobby shuffling came
The lean and faded keeper of the inn,
A wight not old, but rheumatic and lame,
With wrinkled parchment skin, and jet-black eyes

Full of shrewd greed and knowledge of the world ;
And in a voice of harsh and sombre cheer
He croak'd, ' Despair, show in the gentleman—
Methinks another Pilgrim from the City ?
Thy servant, sir! Alack, how wet thou art!—
No night for man or beast to be abroad.
Ho there! more faggots in the supper-room,
The gentleman is cold; but charily, wench,
No waste, no waste, for firewood groweth dear,
And these be pinching times.'
       So saying, he rubb'd
His feeble hands together, chuckling low
A sordid welcome, while a shudder ran,
Half pain, half pity, through my chilly veins,
To see the lean old body clad in rags—
A dreary host, methought; and as I thought,
I glanced around me on the great dark walls
All hung with worm-eat tapestry that stirr'd
In the chill airs that crept about the house;
For through great crannies in the old inn's walls
Came wind and wet, and oftentimes the place
Shook with the blast.
      ' How callest thou thine inn ? '
I ask'd, still shaking off the clammy rain
And stamping on the chilly paven floor—
' Methinks 'tis very ancient ? '

                        'Yea, indeed,'
Answer'd that lean and grim anatomy;
'None older in the land—an ancient house,
Good sir, from immemorial time an inn.
Thou sawest the sign—a skull enwrought with roses,
And wrought into a wine-cup ruby rimm'd?
My father's father's father set it there.'

THE PILGRIM.

Thou seemest full of guests. Thine inn must thrive.

HOST.

Thrive? yea, with thrift! We lie too far away,
Too lone i' the waste, for many travellers;
And they who come, good lack, are mostly poor,
Penniless men with burthens on their backs
And little in their pouches, save us all!
Once on a time, in my good grandsire's day,
The house throve well, and at that very door
King Cruel and full many a mighty man
Lighted, a-hunting here upon the waste.
But now the house decays. Alack, alack!
Sometimes methinks 'twill fall about mine ears.
What then? I have no kin to leave it to,
And if it lasts my little lapse of time

Why, I shall be content ! '
                    Thus murmur'd he,
Ushering into a mighty bed-chamber
His shivering guest; and on the hearth thereof
The marble maid strew'd firewood down and sought
To light a fire, but all the wood was wet,
And with her cold thin lips she blew the flame
To make it glow, while mine host chatter'd on.

' This, master, is the only empty room—
Kept mostly for great guests, but since the house
Is full, 'tis thine. Upon that very bed
King Cruel himself hath slept, and good Priest
       Guile
Before they made him Pope. I'll leave thee, sir.
When thou art ready thou shalt sup below
In pleasant company.'
                    Then methought within
That antique room I stood alone and dried
My raiment at the faint and flickering fire ;
And in the chill blue candlelight the room
Loom'd with vast shadows of the lonely bed,
The heavy hangings, and dim tapestries ;
And there were painted pictures on the walls,
Old portraits, faint and scarce distinguishable
With very age—of monarchs in their crowns,

Imperial victors filleted with bay,
And pallid queens. 'A melancholy place,'
I murmur'd; 'yet 'tis better than the storm
That wails without!'

     Down through that house forlorn
I wended, till I reach'd a festal room,
Oak-panel'd, lighted with a pleasant fire,
And therewithin a supper-table spread
With bakemeats cold, chill cates, and weak wan
  wines.
There, waited on by that pale handmaiden,
I supp'd amid a silent company
Of travellers, for no man spake a word.
But when the board was clear'd and drinks wer
  served,
Around the faggot fire all drew their seats;
And stealing in, a tankard in his hand,
The host made one, and fondled his thin knees.
And now I had leisure calmly to survey
My still companions looming like to ghosts
In the red firelight of the lonely inn.

They seem'd of every clime beneath the sun,
And clad in every garb, but all, it seem'd,
Were melancholy men, and some in sooth

Were less than shadows, houseless and forlorn;
And in the eyes of most was dim desire
And dumb despair; and upon one another
They scarcely gazed, but in the dreary fire
Look'd seeking faces. For a time their hearts,
In the dim silence of that dreary room,
Tick'd audibly, like a company of clocks,
But soon the host upspake, and sought to spread
A feeble cheer.
                'Come, gentlemen, be merry!
More faggots—strew them on the hearth, Despair!
All here are friends and Pilgrims; let's be merry!'
And turning round to one who by his dress
And grizzled beard did seem a travelling Jew,
He added, 'Master Isaac, thou art dull!
What cheer i' the town to-day? How thriveth
    trade?'

'Ill, master,' answer'd, with his heavy eyes
Still on the fire, the Jew itinerant:
'The accursed of Canaan in the temples reign,
And he who by the God of Judah swears
Hath little thrift. I saw a merry sight:
Another Pilgrim stoned for following
The dream their Master, the dead Nazarene,
Preach'd for a sign. Could he not hold his peace,

And smile, as *I* do, spitting o'er my head
In secret, for a curse upon the place?'

Even as he spake I started, listening,
As if I heard the sound of mine own name,
But ere my lips could speak, another voice
Came from the circle, shrill and petulant:

'I saw the sight, and laugh'd with aching sides.
They would have let an atheist pass in peace,
But him they stoned. Poor fool! he went in rags,
Seeking the moonshine City those same priests
Preach, laughing in their sleeves.'
                    A dreary laugh
Ran through the circle as he spoke, but none
Lifted his vacant vision from the fire.
Then I, now glancing at the speaker's face,
Cold, calm, and bitter, lighted with a sneer,
Answer'd—
            'I am that man of whom you speak—
What moves thy mirth?'
                    'Thy folly,' grimly said
The other; and the circle laugh'd again.
But with a cunning and insidious smile
The Jew cried, interposing, 'Softly, friends!
Be civil to the gentleman, who is

A rebel like yourselves, hating as much
Those cruel scarecrows of authority.'
Then, turning with a crafty look to me,
He added quietly—' Thy pardon, sir!
A Pilgrim unto Dreamland, I perceive?'

Whereat I answer'd, frowning sullenly—
' Nay, to the tomb! And as I live, meseems,
In this lone hostel's black sarcophagus,
I reach my journey's end, and stand amid
My fellow corpses!'

                        As I spake the word,
There started up out of that company
A youth with wild large eyes and hair like
     straw,
Lean as some creature from the sepulchre,
The firelight flashing on his hueless cheeks,
Waving his arms above his head, and crying,

'A tomb! it *is* a tomb, and we the dust
Cast down within it—dead! for on our orbs
Falleth no sunlight and no gentle dew,
Nor any baptism shed by Christ or God,
The Phantoms that we follow'd once in quest!
To-day is as to-morrow, and we reck

No touch of Time, but moulder, coffin'd close,
Far from the wholesome stars!'—and as the maid
Pass'd coldly, on her ghastly face he fix'd
His wild, lack-lustre eye: 'Fill, fill, sweet wench;
Let the ghosts sit upon their graves and drink;
And come thou close and sit upon my knee,
That I may kiss thy clammy lips and smooth
Thy chilly golden hair!'
      He sank again,
Fixing his eyes anew upon the fire,
Whilst the Jew whisper'd softly in mine ears:
''Tis Master Deadheart, the mad poet, sir;
Heed not his raving! Once upon a time
He was a Pilgrim like thyself, but now
He dwelleth in the middle of the waste,
Within a dismal castle, ivy-hung
And haunted by the owls.'
      But I replied,
'There's method in his madness. Unto him
God is not, therefore he is surely dead,
And as he saith, a corpse, for God is Life.'

Then spake again he who had laugh'd before
At my dark plight, between his firm-set teeth

Hissing the words and smiling:
                                'Who is this
That prates of God? Another Phantom-hunter!
Another Pilgrim after the All Good,
Who sees not all is evil, even the goad
Of selfish hope that pricks him feebly on?'

The tone was gentler than the words, and
    spake
Pity supreme and sorrow infinite,
Wherefore not angrily did I reply:
'I love to know their names with whom I
    speak,
First tell me thine, and I may answer thee?'

'Why not?' replied the other quietly;
'Our host doth know my name as that of one
That plainly saith his say and pays his score.
My name is Wormwood, and hard by this place
I keep a school for Pilgrims not too old
To learn of me!'

THE PILGRIM.

            Come, school *me* if thou wilt!
Thou sayst that all is evil—prove thy saying.

WORMWOOD.

Why should I prove what thine own simple heart
Is chiming? Prove the sound of funeral bells,
The trump of wars, the moans of martyrdom!
Man, like the beast, is evil utterly,
And man is highest of all things that be.

THE PILGRIM.

Man highest? Aye, of creatures, if thou wilt,
And I will grant he hath an evil heart;
But higher far than Man is very God.

WORMWOOD.

How? Is the Phantom greater than the Fact?
The Shadow than the Substance casting it?

THE PILGRIM.

Not so; and therefore God is more than Man.

WORMWOOD.

Wrong at the catch — for Man is more than God;
For out of Man, the creature of Man's heart,
Colossal image of Man's entity,
Comes God; and therefore, friend, thou followest
Thine own dark shadow which thou deem'st divine,
And since Man's heart is evil (as indeed

Thou hast admitted now in fair round speech),
Evil is God whom thou imaginest!

The speaker laugh'd, and of that company
Many laugh'd too, and I was answering him,
When suddenly a hollow voice exclaim'd,
'A song! a song!' and rising from his seat
With flashing eyes the maniac Poet sang:

> I have sought Thee, and not found Thee,
>   I have woo'd Thee, and not won Thee—
> Wrap Thy gloomy veil around Thee,
>   Keep Thy starry mantle on Thee—
> I am chamber'd far below Thee,
> And I seek no more to know Thee.
>
> Of my lips are made red blossoms;
>   Of my hair long grass is woven;
> From the soft soil of my bosoms
>   Springeth myrrh; my heart is cloven,
> And enrooted there, close clinging,
> Is a blood-red poppy springing.
>
> There is nothing of me wasted,
>   Of my blood sweet dews are fashion'd,
> All is mixed and manifested
>   In a mystery unimpassion'd.
> I am lost and faded wholly,
> Save these eyes, that now close slowly.

And these eyes, though darkly glazing,
    With the spirit that looks through them,
Both before and after gazing
    While the misty rains bedew them,
From the sod still yearn full faintly
For Thy shining soft and saintly.

They are closing, they are shading,
    With the seeing they inherit—
But Thou fadest with their fading,
    Thou art changing, mighty Spirit—
And the end of their soft passion
Is Thine own annihilation!

All join'd the wild refrain, till with the sound
The old inn shook. 'Well sung!' exclaim'd mine host,
And stirr'd the feeble embers of the fire;
And in the calm that follow'd, turning to me,
The Jew smiled quietly and spake again:—

'Good friend, since life is short, and man's heart evil,
And death so near at every path we tread,
Is it not best to clutch the goods we have,
To trade, to barter, and to keep with thrift,
Than to go wandering into mystic lands
Seeking the City that can ne'er be seen?

Put out of sight that bleeding Nazarene
Whose shadow haunts our highways everywhere,
And, faith, the land we dwell in is a land
Gracious and green and pleasant to the eye.
Jew am I, but apostate from the God
Who thunder'd upon Sinai, and indeed
I love no form of thunder, but affect
Calm dealings and smooth greetings with the world.
For this is sure—that we are evil all,
Earth-tainted, man and woman, beast and bird,
We prey on one another, high and low;
And if we cheat ourselves with phantasies,
We miss the little thrift of time we have
And perish ere our prime.'

       ' Most excellent,'
Cried Wormwood; ' *carpe diem*—eat and live—
To-morrow thou shalt die;' and suddenly
He rose and sung a would-be merry tune:

  Pour, Proserpine, thy purple wine
   Into this crystal cup,
  And wreathe my head with poppies red,
   While thus I drink it up.
  Then, marble bride, sit by my side,
   With large eyes fix'd in sorrow,
  To-night we'll feast, and on thy breast
   I'll place my head to-morrow.

> Pale Proserpine, short space is mine
>   To taste the happy hours,
> For thou hast spread my quiet bed,
>   And strewn it deep in flowers.
> O grant me grace a little space,
>   And shroud that face of sorrow,
> Till dawn of day I will be gay,
>   For I'll be thine to-morrow.
>
> Am I not thine, pale Proserpine,
>   My bride with hair of jet?
> Our bridal night is taking flight,
>   But we'll not slumber yet;
> Pour on, pour deep! before I sleep
>   One hour of mirth I'll borrow—
> Upon thy breast, in haggard rest,
>   I'll place my head to-morrow.

He ceased, and stillness on the circle came,
Like silence after thunder, and again
All gazed with dreary eyeballs on the fire.
But now the chill and rainy dawn crept in
And lighted all those faces with its beam.
'To bed!' cried one, and shivering I arose,
And through great lobbies colder than the tomb,
And up great carven stairs with curtains hung,
I follow'd that pale handmaiden, who bare
A chilly wind-blown lamp, until again

I stood within the antique bedchamber,
And setting down the light the maiden fix'd
Her stony eyes on mine and said ' Good-night;'
Then with no sound of footsteps flitted off,
And left me all alone.
                    Long time I paced
The dreary chamber, haunted by the sound
Of mine own footfalls, then I laid me down,
Not praying unto God as theretofore,
In the great bed, and by my bedside set
The rushlight burning low; and all around
The pallid pictures on the mouldering walls
Look'd at me silently and seem'd to smile,
While quietly the great bed's canopy
Outstretch'd in rustling folds above my head.
But as my senses faded one by one
I seem'd to see those pallid Kings and Queens
Descend and flit across the oaken floor
With marble faces and blue rayless eyes;
And that dark canopy above became
A Christ upon His Cross, outstretching arms
And bending down to look into my face
With eyes of dumb, dead, infinite despair.

BOOK VIII.
THE OUTCAST, ESAU.

O DREARY dawn! from drearier dreams I woke,
And found it gently creeping through the pane
And shedding dusky silver on the floor;
Whereon I rose, and slipping down the stairs,
From chilly gallery to gallery,
I stole until I reach'd the ghostly hall;
Yet, early as it was, Host Moth was up
And shivering in his slippers at the door,
For folk were bearing in upon a bier
A ragged woman and her newborn child,
Both dead, found frozen on the waste hard by,
And the lean host was chiding querulously,
Bidding them take their ghastly load elsewhere,
Nor mar his custom with a sight so sad;—
So intent was he, he scarcely seem'd to heed
My greeting, but he clutch'd with eager hand
The reckoning I tost him as I pass'd.

Then out again upon the dreary waste
I passed slow-footed, while a chilly wind
Blew up along the black horizon line
Dusk streaks of crimson like dead burnish'd leaves,
And through their fluttering folds a gusty film
Sparkled and melted into crystal dew.
Then I was 'ware that straight across the waste
There ran a dreary and an open way,
With gloomy reaches of the sunless moor,
And lonely tarns alive with ominous light,
Stretching on either side; and by the tarns
The bittern boom'd and the gray night-hern cried,
And high in air against the dreary gleam
A string of black swans waver'd to the south;
But presently, as the dull daylight grew,
I encounter'd men and women on the road
Coming and going; all were closely wrapt,
With eyes that sought the ground, but some strode by
With frowning brows and haggard sleepless eyes:
A melancholy race they seem'd indeed
Of toilers on the moorland and the marsh.
One I accosted, a tall, woeful man,
Gaunt, clad in rags, and shivering in the cold,
And question'd of the City and whither led
That dreary open way; and for a space
He answer'd not, but as a dumb man tries

With foam-froth'd tongue to gather shreds of speech,
Stood muttering, with his blank eyes gazing at me
In wonder, but at last he found a voice.

THE MAN.

A City, master? Nay, I know of none,
And in this country I was born and bred.

THE PILGRIM.

But whither runs this road across the waste?

THE MAN.

Far as a man may walk until he drops,
And farther, league on league of loneliness,
It leadeth—whither I know not, since my toil
Keepeth me busy here upon the heath;
But yonder to the right a rugged path
Winds to the mountains, where, I have heard, there
    dwells
A race of moonstruck madmen, mountaineers.

THE PILGRIM.

Alas! and toilest thou upon the ground,
Nor seekest to be wandering far away,
Upward and heavenward to the radiant place
Where stands the City of God?

The Man.

                    I know not God,
Nor any City of so strange a name;
Yet I have often heard my granddam tell
(When I was but a child) of some bright place
Where folk might cease their weary work and
    rest;
But, master, she died mad! My father saith,
Who reared me up and made me toil for bread,
That they are mad folk too who pass this way,
Clad like thyself in pilgrim's robes and shoon,
Seeking that City and calling out on God.

I left him standing like a marble man,
With humbled head and heavily hanging brow,
And wander'd on; and when my weary feet
Had gone a little space, I backward gazed,
And saw him gazing dumbly after me
With vacant eyeballs; and the daylight grew;
And many others pass'd with looks as dull,
Faces as blank, and tread as sorrowful,
And all seem'd little cheer'd by the dim dawn,
But crawl'd to some dark taskwork on the waste;
But some that pass'd on horseback carried loads
Of corn and gold, as to some dreary mart.

Deep darkness seal'd mine eyelids for a time,
And when they open'd, opening still in dream,
Amid mysterious shadows drifting by
Confused and imageless, methought my form
Now shone deep hidden, like a stormy moon;
And fast I seem'd to fly, as seems the moon
Through the swift tempest-rack to plough her
    way,
Yet stirs not, but beholds the vaporous drift
Floating and flying round her luminous feet.
Nor could my troubled eyes distinguish well
What land I walk'd in, or to what far bourne
My slow feet fared, though dimly I discern'd
A weary waste it was without a road,
Figure of man, or sign of any star.

Meseem'd that weary years had pass'd away
Since first upon that lonely waste I fared,
For ever struggling, yet for evermore
As stationary as the storm-vex'd moon;
And endless seem'd the heavy space of time.
At last, as in the growing light of day
The night-clouds thin, and in white wreaths of
    smoke,
Soon kindled into crimson, float away,
The shadows that across me darkly stream'd

Grew fainter, melted, brighten'd, and dissolved,
Till every shade was fled, the prospect clear,
And once again I paused upon the path,
Standing and gazing round me, solitary,
'Mid dusky gleams of dawn.

      Now, far away
I saw the flashing of Christopolis
Bright and remote as is a phantom city
Seen in the sunset, and as sunset towers
Crumble to golden vapour and are lost
Strangely and quickly of their own bright will,
So flash'd the holy City's walls and spires
Dissolved by distance. 'Tween Christopolis
And my now lingering feet stretch'd waste on
  waste,
Weary, forlorn, abandon'd, without bound,
With never wood or gentle cynosure,
Or flash of silver stream, or human dwelling,
To break its infinite monotony.
There had I linger'd, thence my feet had fared,
I knew not how; for all the way was dark
Behind me, dim the sense and memory,
And dimly sad; and all my wandering thither
Was like an evil ill-remember'd dream;
Nor yet of that forlornest solitude

My feet were free, for round about me still
Its dreary prospect dawn'd.
                    While thus I stood
Dejected, leaning heavy on my staff,
I faintly heard, far off across the heath,
The sound of horse's hoofs, which ever came
Nearer and nearer; till mine eyes beheld
Approaching, swift as any storm-swept cloud,
A horseman with his wild hair backward streaming,
His hands outreaching o'er his horse's mane;
Quickly he came, and from the ground beneath
Shot sparks of fire, for mighty was his steed
Beyond all common steeds that stride the earth,
Maned like a comet, and as black as clouds
That blot a comet's path;
And though its back was bare and 'tween its
    teeth
It bare no bit, most tamely it obey'd
The white hand twisted in its trembling mane;
And ever with its bright eye backward flashing
Neigh'd to the murmur of its rider's mouth,
And ever sprang more swiftly on and on
The more his hand caress'd. Onward it came;
And now I saw that he who strode the steed
Was slight and white and woman-like of form,
Though on his pallid cheek there burn'd resolve

Of mighty men; and his blue eye was fix'd
On vacancy, so that he noted not
The figure of the Pilgrim on his way;
And he was flashing past with fair face set
Like any star, when with one mighty bound
The steed leapt back, its nostrils flashing fire,
And striking up the sward with horny hoofs
Stood quivering. Starting from his trance, like one
Shaken from quiet sleep, the rider turn'd
His face on mine, and, lo, that face was stern
In pallor, and his dove-like eye became
Keen as an eagle's fix'd upon its prey.
'What man art thou?' he question'd; and I
    said,
Dejected, sick from very weariness,
Scarce lifting up my head, 'See for thyself!
A Pilgrim well-nigh spent!'
                    The horseman's face
Grew brighter, though he laugh'd a bitter laugh,
Then leaping from his seat but holding still
His black steed's mane, quickly across the ground
He pass'd, and coming close he gazed for long
Into my face; then lightly laugh'd again,
Saying, 'Well met! Methinks I know thee now,
Or else thy dreary cheek belies thy soul—
Thou comest from Christopolis! How now?

The Outcast, Esau.

Hast thou been stoned i' the town, and have thy
    robes
Been rent, and thou cast forth beyond the gate ?
Answer, and fear not! I who question thus
Am outcast like thyself.'
                        Then did I tell,
In hurried accents panting out my pain,
My hope, my dream, my weary life-long quest,
And all my sorrow in Christopolis;
And how for many days and nights my feet
Had struggled in the darkness of the waste;
And how my light was lost, my strength nigh
    spent,
My path all solitary; yea, how no Christ
Could bring me comfort, and no God at all
Could bring me peace—'Because,' I murmur'd
    low,
'My heart is dead!'
                      Again that stranger laugh'd,
And, answering him, the jet-black steed threw up
His head and through great nostrils neigh'd aloud.
Then cried he, 'Toiler on the ground, too low
Thou crawlest, even as a creeping thing.
But knowest thou *me?*' Whereon I answer'd,
    'Nay,'
And looking up more eagerly, beheld

The light of starry eyes that shook with dew
Of their exceeding lustre, wondrously.

Then the clear voice, in accents sweet as song,
Cried, 'Christ they crucified, and thee they
    stoned,
And me they would have given to the fire—
Esau am I, call'd even after him
Whom smooth sly Jacob of his birthright robb'd
In times of old. Another Jacob sits
In the high places of Christopolis,
Eating my substance. Long ago I rode
Into their Temples, overcasting them
Who at the bloody altars minister'd;
And in their market-places I proclaim'd
Their god an idol and their creed a lie;
And in the madness of mine own despair
Wassail I held, with lemans at my side,
In the dark centre of their midmost shrine,
And there they found me and shrieking "Anti-
    Christ!"
They would have slain me, but my steed was nigh,
And on his back I sprang with laugh full shrill,
Trampled their priests as dust beneath my feet,
And through their dark throngs plunged, till once
    again

On the fair waste I wander'd.'

       Then I said,
' Where dwellest thou ? '
       ' Where doth the swift wind dwell,
That on the high places and on the low,
Homeless for ever, ever is found and lost?
Even as the wind am I; the lonely woods,
The torrents, the great solitary meres,
Know me, and through their solitude I sail
Even as amid the tempest sails the crane.
All these have voices, crying as I pass
Compassionless, alone ; and from their speech
And silent looks I have drunk deeper joy
Than ever in any temple rear'd by hands
The soul of man hath known. Wilt ride with me ?
O Pilgrim, wilt thou ride ? '
       So saying, he sprang
Again upon his mighty sinewy steed,
Which leapt for very joy beneath his weight,
And holding out his white hand eagerly,
He murmur'd, ' Come ! ' Then cried I, hesitating,
' But whither ? Knowest thou that fair City I seek,
Or any place of peace ? '
       ' Ask not, but come,'
Answer'd that other, while his black steed rear'd
In act to paw the air and bound along—

And ere I knew it I had ta'en the hand,
And leaping on the steed was clinging tight
To that pale horseman, who with wild laugh
    cried,
' Away ! away ! '
                As from a tense-strung bow
Whistles the wingèd shaft, or as a star
Shoots into space, the sable steed upleapt
And bounded on ; so swift its fiery speed,
That to its rider pale I clung in fear,
While underneath I saw the billowy heath
Rush by me like a boiling whirling tide.
I seem'd as one uplifted high in air,
Sailing through ever-drifting clouds, between
The regions of the flower and of the star,
And for a time my head swam dizzily
And in a trance of speed I closed mine eyes.
Then in mine ears I seem'd to hear the rush
Of many winds, the cry of many streams,
The crash of many clouds ; yet evermore
I felt the beating of the horse's hoofs
Beneath me, and its breathing like the sound
Of fire blown from a forge.
                        At first my soul
Shrunk trembling, but betimes a new desire
Uprose within my heart and in mine eyes

Soon sparkled while they open'd gazing round;
And I beheld with wild ecstatic thrills
New prospects flashing past as dark as dream:
For through a mighty wood of firs and pines
Shapen like harps, wherefrom the rising wind
Drew wails of wild and wondrous melody,
The steed was speeding; and the stars had risen,
Cold-sparkling through the jet-black naked boughs;
And far before us in our headlong track
Great torrents flash'd round gash'd and gaunt
    ravines;
And higher glimmer'd rocks and crags and peaks,
O'er which, with blood-red beams, 'mid driving
    clouds
The windy moon was rising.
                            Once again,
I question'd, looking on the rider's face
Which glimmer'd in the moonlight dim as death,
'Whither, O whither?'
                            And the answer came,
Not in cold speech or chilly undertone,
But musically, in a wild strange song,
To which the sobbing of the torrents round,
The moaning of the wind among the pines,
The beating of the horse's thunderous feet,
Kept strange accord.

Winds of the mountain, mingle with my crying,
Clouds of the tempest, flee as I am flying,
Gods of the cloudland, Christus and Apollo,
    Follow, O follow!

Through the dark valleys, up the misty mountains,
Over the black wastes, past the gleaming fountains,
Praying not, hoping not, resting nor abiding,
    Lo, I am riding!

Who now shall name me? who shall find and bind me?
Daylight before me, and darkness behind me,
E'en as a black crane down the winds of heaven
    Fast I am driven.

Clangour and anger of elements are round me,
Torture has clasp'd me, cruelty has crown'd me,
Sorrow awaits me, Death is waiting with her—
    Fast speed I thither!

Not 'neath the greenwood, not where roses blossom,
Not on the green vale on a loving bosom,
Not on the sea-sands, not across the billow,
    Seek I a pillow!

Gods of the storm-cloud, drifting darkly yonder,
Point fiery hands and mock me as I wander,
Gods of the forest glimmer out upon me,
    Shrink back and shun me!

Gods, let them follow!—gods, for I defy them!
They call me, mock me; but I gallop by them—
If they would find me, touch me, whisper to me,
    Let them pursue me!

Faster, O faster! Darker and more dreary
Groweth the pathway, yet I am not weary—
Gods, I defy them! gods, I can unmake them,
    Bruise them and break them!

White steed of wonder, with thy feet of thunder,
Find out their temples, tread their high-priests under,—
Leave them behind thee—if their gods speed after,
    Mock them with laughter.

Who standeth yonder, in white raiment reaching
Down to His bare feet? who stands there beseeching?
Hark how He crieth, beck'ning with his finger,
    'Linger, O linger!'

Shall a god grieve me? shall a phantom win me?
Nay—by the wild wind around and o'er and in me—
Be his name Vishnu, Christus, or Apollo—
    Let the god follow!

Clangour and anger of elements are round me,
Torture has clasp'd me, cruelty has crown'd me,
Sorrow awaits me, Death is waiting with her—
    Fast speed I thither!

And as the singer sang,
Dark hooded creatures, moving through the woods
In black processions, paused and echoed him;
And on their faces fell the livid light,
While to the wind-blown boughs they lifted hands;
And from the torrent's bed a spirit shriek'd
With eldritch cry. Still the black steed plunged on,
And as it went it seem'd that spectral hands
Were stretch'd to tear its rider from his seat,
But laughing low he urged his eager steed,
And from his beauty those frail phantoms fell
Like flakes of cloud blown into gleaming air
By the soft breathing of some patient star.
Then upward, through the desolate ravines,
Past flashing cataracts and torrent pools,
Along dim ledges that in silence lean'd
O'er horrible abysses dimly lit
By mirror'd moons, the horseman held his way,
Until he came unto a lonely sward
As bright and green as verdure softly trod
By elfin feet, which high among the crags
Stretch'd in the moonlight. Like some abbey old
Around whose crumbling walls and buttresses
The ivy frosted white by moonlight twines,
And whose deep floor of deep green grass is rough
With fragments of old shrines and mossy graves,

This lone spot seem'd; for round the stone-strewn
    grass
The dark crags rose like builded walls and towers
All dark and desolate and ivy twined,
And through the open arches overhead
The moon and stars shone in.
                              Here from his seat,
(While I, too, leapt upon the grassy ground,)
Dark Esau lighted, and relinquishing
His grasp upon the mighty horse's mane,
Cried: 'Feed thy fill!' and o'er the silvern
    grass,
Casting a shade gigantic, slowly walk'd
The black steed, feeding gently as it went.
'Behold my Temple!' upward pointing cried
That pallid wanderer—'hark how the wind
Intoneth with deep organ-voice amid
These ivied lofts, and see how wondrously
With spectral hand that white moon lifts the
    Host!
Hither, when I am sick of wandering
Like some dark spirit up and down the earth,
I come by night, and pant my passing prayer
To Him who made the tempest which ere long
Shall gnaw the heartstrings of Christopolis!
Hither the white Christ comes not, nor His priests,

Nor any feet of slaves; and here thy soul
May rest a space and worship at its will
Whatever god thou choosest, or indeed,
May make an idol of its own despair,
And kneeling, pray to *that!*'
                            The wild wind wail'd,
The dark clouds drifted even as driving waves
Over the moon, while 'mid the ivied crags
The screech-owl cried. Then said I, shivering,
Yet feeling still my eager heart abeat
With all the ecstasy of that mad ride,
' Most cheerless is thy Temple!—and its god
Only the god o' the storm!'
                            ' Cheerless, perchance,'
Answer'd the outcast one, ' yet not unblest—
For lo! 'tis gentle, and its altar-stones
Cemented are with no poor innocent blooa
Drawn from the throat of lambs or lamb-.ike
        men;
And from its porches Lazarus is not driven;
And in its inmost shrines the priests of Baal
Are not upheaping gold. Better such cheer,
Though bitter as the bruisèd heart of Love,
Than merry music of a thousand choirs
Drowning the moans of sad humanity;
Than glory of a thousand golden shrines,

Each one of which shuts up within its folds
A thousand hearts still beating and still bleeding!
This is my Temple; and its god, thou sayst,
Is but the Storm-god?—Blessings on that god!
Upon his burning eyes and night-black hair,
His dark breath and the fire around his feet!
For rock'd in his wild arms the soul of man
May find the comfort of divine unrest.
O, who could dwell upon the dreary earth,
Hark to the wretched wailing, and behold
The terror and the anarchy of Nature,
And keep his heart from breaking, did he never
Upleap and rush into the whirl of things,
And like a wild cloud driven up and down
Ease the mad motion of his life in tears?
My Storm-god—hear him cry! my god o' the
    winds,
List to him, list!—for as he murmureth there
He murmur'd to the wind-blown tribes o' the
    Jew!—
More holy he than yonder hungry Lamb,
Who, pale and impotent in gentleness,
Sits in His niche complacent and beholds
Those hecatombs of broken hearts which priests,
In blood-red robes adjusted smilingly,
Pile on His altars!'

                    All erect he stood,
Pale as an angel in the white-heat gleam
Of Heaven's central sun, and from his eyes
Gleam'd light now lovely and now terrible;
And in the cloudy wrack above his head
Answer'd the Storm-god with a clangour of wind
Like far-off thunder.
                        Silent for a space
I waited, for the words within my heart
Woke awful echoes, but at last I spake,
Saying: 'Yea, there is wisdom in thy words—
Better to wander up and down the world
All outcast, or in Nature's stormy fanes
To pray in protestation and despair,
Than in Christopolis with priests and slaves
To gnaw the frozen crust of a cold creed
Amid the brazen glory of a lie.
Yet am I weary of much storm, and fain
To rest by quiet waters. Blest be thou,
If thou canst guide me thither.'
                            Passionately
The wanderer laugh'd, brushing with thin white
        hand
The long hair blown into his burning eyes—
'By quiet waters? I have search'd the world
And found them not; yea, not from Zion hill,

Nor from the brighter sides of Helicon,
Such waters flow;—and all that I have seen
Are stony to the sight, and to the taste
Most bitter!'
　　　　　　'Woe is me! If this be so,
Where shall we rest our feet?'
　　　　　　　　　　'Rest not at all,'
He answer'd. 'Doth the cloud rest, or the stream,
Or sun, or star, or any shape that moves
Still onward, by its dim will piloted,
As solitary as the soul of man?
Be thou a meteor blown from place to place,
Still testifying up and down the earth
Against the power that made thee miserable;
Then die! soul-sure thou hast not lived in vain,
If with thy hand ere dying thou hast smitten
Some hateful Altar down!'
　　　　　　　Then did I cry,
In darkness and in agony and despair:
'O misery! Is there no light at all
To guide my footsteps on? What country lies
Beyond these hills?'
　　　　　　Answer'd the Wanderer:
'A land of Shepherds—in the vales beyond
The flocks of Faunus feed.—Why, how thy face
Is shining!'

THE PILGRIM.

    Lead me thither—very sweet
The name is, and methinks the land is fair.
A shepherd there 'mong shepherds I will hear
The brook flow, see the sheep upon the heights
Trickling like silvern streams;—and, if I can,
Forget mine own mad quest.

ESAU.

       Mount, if thou wilt,
And I will lead thee thither; but remember
They knee strange gods.

THE PILGRIM.

    Strange gods?

ESAU.

       Yea, strange and dead.
Still bleeding, with a dove upon his lips,
Down its bright streams the slain Adonis floats;
'Mid its deep umbrage Faunus lies his length
Strewn by the robin redbreast and the wren
With gentle leaves; and in some dumb, dark mere,
With all the lustrous ooze about his hair,
Lies drownéd Pan!

The Pilgrim

    Sweet gods! I know them well.
Surely the land wherein they sleep is blest,
A land of peace; surely thy stormy soul
Might there have found its place of rest?

Esau.

         The dead
Shall never have *my* worship! Fair indeed
The land is, and amid its woods and vales
A space I wander'd, till its flowery breath,
Rich as the breathing of a summer rose,
Oppress'd my soul to swooning. So again
I rode into the tempest of the world!
Better to be weariest-wingéd cloud
That to and fro about the shoreless heaven
Flieth without a spot to rest its feet;
Better to be the weariest wave that breaks
Moaning and dying on Thought's shoreless sea,
Than the supremest blossom born i' the wood
And like a snow-flake shed upon the ground!
Oh, I have rested in a hundred bowers,
And should have dream'd to death a thousand times,
But that the clarion of mine own despair
Found me and woke me. For this head of mine

Earth finds no pillow!—I have cradled it
On breasts of women warm with wildest love,
And sighing low, 'Here is my heaven at last,'
I have sunken down into delicious sleep;
But lo! the very billowing of those breasts,
The very come-and-go of Love's own heart,
Hath waken'd me!—with every hot pulse beating
I have risen, and, upspringing to my feet,
Heard the far trumpet blowing!

       As he spake,
His face flash'd like a star, and, raising hands
To the dark, dripping wrack above his head,
He trembled as a tree in the mad wind
Of his wild words; then whistling to his steed,—
Which came unto him tame as any hound,
With foot that paw'd the ground and eyes of fire,—
He cried: 'To horse; and onward!'

        To his seat
Smiling he leapt, and, hesitating not,
I follow'd, clinging round his slender waist
With eager hands; and swiftly once again
The lonely ride began.

      Meseem'd we rode
For many nights and days, yet day and night
Were strangely mingled, and my senses lost

True count of time. Through desolate ravines,
O'er lonely mountain-peaks, and down the beds
Of vanish'd torrents, our strange pathway lay;
And fleeter than the feet of swift izzards
That twinkle on the Pyrenean crags
Where never man may creep or sheep may crawl,
The feet of that swift steed, from spot to spot,
Moved, never slipping and for ever sure.
Ever above us moan'd the winds and moved
The clouds wind-driven; ever with low voice
Dark Esau sang; and in his songs he named
The death-star and the birth-star and the signs
Of Adam, and of Christ, and Antichrist;
And sometimes of dark woods and waters wild,
And of the snow upon the mountain-tops,
He wove wild runes, and scatter'd them like
    flowers
Under the trampling footsteps of the storm.

So rode we on and on. At last, meseem'd
The pace grew slower, the steed's fiery breath
More gentle, while upon my face there fell
A warmth like sunlight. Gazing round, I saw
That we were riding down a green hillside,
Flowers and grass were growing underfoot,
The summer sun was shining, and a lark

Uprose before the horse's very feet,
Singing !
    Still slower grew the dark steed's pace,
And now upon the brightening sward his hoofs
Fell soft as fruit that falleth from the bough ;
While Esau, ceasing his mad minstrelsy,
Relax'd his hold upon the flowing mane,
And with his chin sunk forward on his breast,
Frown'd darkly, in a dream.

        Beneath us lay
A mighty Valley, darken'd everywhere
With woods primæval, whose umbrageous tops
Roll'd with the great wind darkly, like a sea ;
And waves of shadow travell'd softly on
Far as the eye could see across the boughs,
And upward came a murmur deep and sweet,
Such as he hears who stands on ocean sands
On some divine, dark day of emerald calm.
And when we rode into the greenness stretch'd
Beneath us, and along the dappled shades
Crept slowly on a carpet mossy and dark,
It seemëd still as if with charmëd lives
We walk'd some wondrous bottom of the Deep.
For pallid flowers and mighty purple weeds,
Such as bestrew the Ocean, round us grew,

Soft stirring as with motions of the ooze;
And far above, the boughs did break like waves
To foam of flowers and sunlight, with a sound
Solemn, afar off, faint as in a dream!

Now ever lull'd by that deep melody,
Dark Esau held his chin upon his breast,
And gazing neither right nor left, rode on
With deeper frown. So stole we slowly on
Through that green shade.
      Suddenly on our ears
There came a sound of sylvan melody,
Deep, like the lover's lute; and 'mid that sound
A voice rose clear and sparkling as a fountain
Upleaping from some nest of greenery.
Dark Esau raised his head, and his twain eyes
Grew luminous as any serpent's orbs,
Watching a space of sunlight bright as gold
Which open'd through the boughs before his path.
And soon meseem'd into that sunny space
Slowly he rode, and dazzled in the gleam,
Stood glorified and shading both his brows;
And there, beside the sparkle of a stream, .
I saw a Shepherd and a Shepherdess
Sit smiling; and upon a shepherd's pipe
The wight play'd soft and low, while loud and clear,

Sitting and clasping hands around her knees,
And gazing at the glimmer overhead,
The Maiden sang!
                    Dark were the Shepherd's locks,
Threaded with silvern grey, and on his face
A brownness as of ripen'd fruitage lay;
And though the fever of his youth was past,
His black eyes flash'd with some deep inner fire
Wherein his heart was burning. O'er his brow
A fillet green he wore; around his form
A mantle azure as the open heaven,
And wrought with lilies like to heavenly stars;
Dark shoon upon his feet, and by his side
There lay a gentle crook Arcadian.
Him did I quickliest mark, and whisper'd low:
'What wight is he that plays?'—and Esau said,
Now smiling darkly and in mockery:
'Thyrsis, the shepherd of the flocks of Faun;
He saw Diana pass one summer night
In all the wonder of her nakedness.
He was a boy then, but his hair that hour
Was silver'd; since that hour he hath not smiled,
But on his cheek the wonder of that sight
Still flashes flame!' He added, while his eye
Kindled to feverish rapture: 'Turn thine eyes
On her who sings beside him in the sun!

Was ever hamadryad half so fair?
He found her even like any fallen flower
In the warm heart o' the wood one summer night,
And wanton spirits whisper'd in his ear
That she was Dian's child. He took the babe,
And rear'd her as his own; and there she sits
Fairer than Dian's self!'
                      Fairer, indeed,
Than any woman of a woman born
Was that strange Shepherdess. Her face was bright
As sunlight, but her lips were poppy-red,
And o'er her brows and alabaster limbs
The lilies and the roses interblent
In that full glory. Raven-black her hair,
And black her brows o'er azure eyes that swam
With passionate and never-ceasing fires
Deep hidden 'neath her snows; most brilliantly
They burnt, but with no trembling, fitful light,
Nay, rather, steady as two vestal stars;
And though their flame was passionately bright,
Soul-'trancing, soul-consuming, yet it seem'd
Most virginal and sweetly terrible,
Chaste with the splendour of an appetite
That never could be fed on food of earth,
Or stoop to quench its chastity with less
Than perfect godhead.

As the steed drew near,
She ceased her song, and fix'd on Esau's face
Her melting eyes; and paler than the dead
He turn'd, his lips like ashes, and his hand
Held heavily on his heart. She did not stir,
Nor smile, nor did her shining features change;
But quietly the elder Shepherd rose
And stood erect, but leaning on his crook
In silence, while dark Esau, with a smile,
Grim as the smile upon a corpse's face,
Forced from his heart a hollow laugh, and cried:
' Ho, Thyrsis! see, what guest I bring to thee!
Another Pilgrim sick of Christ and God,
And eager for the clammy kiss of Earth—
Aye, or content, if thou wilt have it so,
To sleep on Dian's breast!'

       The Shepherd raised
His hand in deprecation, answering low:
' Blaspheme not, Esau! she thou namest is
Too holy for thy lips!'—then courteously
Turning to me, who now upon the grass
Had leapt with eager feet, he bow'd his head,
Saying, ' Be welcome! May thy soul find rest
In these green shades!'

       But Esau, with his eyes
Still fix'd upon the maiden feverishly,

Echoed him: 'Rest! God help him! Rest with
    thee?'
'Why not?' the Shepherd said, not angrily,
But softly as the rippling runlet falls.
The other answer'd not, but laugh'd aloud,
And pointed with his fingers mockingly
At the pale Maiden, who unto her feet
Rose like a spirit, shining, with no sound.

Then Esau cried, with quick laugh like a shriek,
'Away!'—and as the laughter left his lips,
The steed sprang on across the golden glade
And plunged into the umbrage suddenly;
But ere it faded Esau's pallid face
Cast one last look behind on her who shone
Still as a star.
        Softly the Shepherd sigh'd,
And to the questioning look upon my face
Made answer: 'Dian, give that wanderer peace!
None other, god or goddess, ever can!
I see thou marvellest much at his wild words,
And wilder looks.—Sir, 'tis the old, sad tale.
He loved my child, whom I in reverence
Named Dian, after Dian the divine,
The holy ministress of these dark woods.
He loved her, as full many a wight hath done,

But never upon any man that lives
She smileth, and methinks the good gods will
That she shall die a maid!'

       Then did my soul
Marvel in sooth to hear the names of gods
Falling so simply from the Shepherd's tongue;—
For reverently, with lowly-lidded eyne,
The Shepherd spake, and reverently his child
Gazed upward, like to one who seeth afar
The dewy star-point of an angel's wing.
Wherefore I murmur'd, half to those who heard,
Half to myself: 'Gods!—but the gods are
  dead!'
And Thyrsis answer'd: 'As the pallid Christ,
Swathen in burial linen icy cold,
Sepulchred deep, and sealéd with a stone,
Yet walking from His grave, and withering
The grass of centuries with feet of fire,
As He is dead, so they! If He abides,
They are not lost!—and though the eye of Faith
Hath grown too dim to trace their forms divine,
The gods survive, heirs of their own green realm,
Inheritors of immortality!
For this is fatal:—to be beautiful,
Is to be thrice divine, as Dian is!'

And as he named the blessed name again
His face shone with its pale beatitude.

' But come !' he cried—' dwell with us for a space,
And I will guide thee through our woodland realm,
And tell thee of its secrets one by one.
The fever of the world is on thy face,
The wormwood of the Priest is on thy heart;
And here by quiet waters thou shalt brood
On shapes of beauty till thy thought becomes
As beautiful as that it broodeth on.'

He ceased; I answer'd not; my soul was wrapt
In contemplation of the flower-crown'd Maid,
Who turning on me, softly as a star
Opens in heaven, all the dreamful light
Of her still face, stood gazing into mine
With all the wonder of immortal eyes
Tremulous with unutterable desire
That never could be fed. Then, even as one
Under enchantment, spell-bound by that face,
Still gazing on it in a burning awe,
In a low voice I answer'd, ' I will stay !'

BOOK IX.

THE GROVES OF FAUN.

STILL listening to that stately Eremite,
And gently gazing on the snowy Maid
Who glided on before us golden-hair'd,
We pass'd into a mighty forest grove,
When on mine eager ears there swept a sound
Of birds innumerable on leafy boughs
Singing aloud !—and as we softly trod
The mossy carpet of the broad bright glade,
With trees of ancient growth on either side,
We suddenly beheld a group of forms,
That, clustering before us on the sward,
With large, brown, lustrous eyes fix'd full on ours,
Stood like a startled flock of fallow-deer
Prepared to spring away ; yet shaped like men
Were these, though hairy were their limbs, their feet
Cloven like feet of swine, and all their ears,
That large and hairy twinkled in the sun,
Prick'd up to listen. Golden shone the light
Upon them, and their shadows on the sward

Were softly strewn, as thither with quick cry
Hasten'd the Maid; but, ere into their midst
Her feet could spring, they ev'n as startled deer
Leapt, flitted, vanish'd, with a faint, wild cry,
Like human laughter on a hill-top heard,
Forlorn and indistinct; but as their shapes
Vanish'd afar, deep down the emerald glade
A thousand sylvan echoes answer'd them,
And from the leaves on either side the way
Innumerable faces flash'd, as fair
As ever wood-nymph wore. Then did I know
Those glades were haunted by the flocks of Faun;
The Satyr dwelt there, and the Sylvan throng,
And in the wood's hot heart the Naïad fill'd
The hollow of her white outstretchèd hand
With drops of summer dew.

       And as I went
I gladden'd more; for never groves of earth
Were half so fair as those wherein I trod.
Statues of marble, mystically wrought,
Gleam'd in the open spaces cool and white
As shapes of snow; and here and there were strewn
The ruin'd steps of marble white and red,
Or broken marble columns moss-bestain'd,
That show'd where once a Temple had been raised

To Pan or Faunus, or some lesser god
Of wood or stream; and though those temples fair
Were overthrown, the Spirits unto whom
They had been raised were there, and merry amid
The ruins of the shrine.

       'I know them well,'
I murmur'd, smiling, ' these enchanted groves,
Where Faunus leads his legions ruminant;
And where Selene, with soft silvern feet,
Walks every summer night; and well I know
They are but conjurations of the sense
Which sees them—shadows, neither less nor more,
Of Nature's primal joy.'

       The Shepherd smiled,
And said: 'The substance, not the shadow. These,
And all such joyous images as these,
Are elemental—weary were the world
Whence they were wholly flown. Once on a time
They peopled the wide earth, and man might mark
At every roadside, and by every door,
Flower-crown'd Priapus, the fair child of Pan,
Close kin to Love and Death; but now they haunt
Only the places of the solitude
Where mortals seldom creep. Seen or unseen,
Known or unknown, they are immortal, part

Of that eternal youth and happiness
Which first created them, and whence they draw
Their brightness and their being.'

       Silently
We wander'd on, and now our footsteps fell
In scented shade. From every nook i' the leaves
A Spirit peep'd; o'erhead from every bough
A Spirit sang!—and ever and anon,
Out of the flower-enwoven and emerald gloom,
White arms were waved, while voices soft as sleep
Did whisper, 'Come!' Calm through the throng-
  ing flowers
Whose honey'd sweets were crushed against his lips,
The Shepherd trod. The bright light fell subdued
Upon the snow of his divine grey hair,
And every woodland Spirit that upsprang
To clasp him in her warm and naked arms,
Gazed for a moment in his solemn eyes,
Then like a fountain falling sank in shame
To kiss his feet. The marble Maiden moved
Untouch'd by any of the glittering beams,
Pure as a dewdrop the light gleams upon
Yet cannot drink, while lost in light my soul
Sprang from its sheath of sorrow, and in the sun
Hover'd like any golden butterfly!

I leapt i' the joyful air, I laugh'd aloud,
I stretch'd mine arms to every flashing form,
I kiss'd fair faces fading into flowers,
I drank the sunshine down like golden wine;
And, lastly, sinking on a rainbow'd bank,
O'er-canopied by faces, forms, and eyes,
That changed and changed to radiant fruit and flowers
With every breathing of the summer wind,
I cried, ' Farewell! Leave me to linger here.
My quest was vain, but oh, these bowers are blest!
I'll roam no further!'

      ' Rise!' the old man said;
'Who linger in these vales of vain delight
Perish betimes; it is thy privilege
To share as doth a master, not a slave,
Fair Nature's primal joy! On every side
See scatter'd those who lie too wholly lost
Ever to rise again.' And all around,
Across the tangled paths on every side,
I saw indeed that many mortal shapes
Were fallen like o'er-ripe fruit; and many of these
Were clad as if for heavenly pilgrimage,
Yea, arm'd with staff and scrip; but o'er them bent
Women so lustrous and so sweetly pale
They seem'd of marble and moonlight interblent,

And yet so bright and warm in nakedness
They seem'd of living flesh. Ah, God, to see
Their syren faces, dead-eyed like the Sphynx,
Yet lustrous-cheek'd, with bright vermilion lips
Like poppy-flowers! Yet sadder still than theirs
The faces that below them on the grass
Flash'd amorous of the very breath they drew!
Pale youths and students Time had snow'd upon ;
Gaunt poets, clasping to their cold breast-bones
Their harps of gold ; and hunters, clad in green,
Gross-mouth'd and lewd ; and kings, that proffer'd
        crowns
For one cold kiss ; and senile agéd men,
Who shook like palsied leaves upon the tree
With every thrill of sylvan melody
That breathed beneath the overhanging boughs.
These things beholding, to my feet I sprang
With piteous cry, and as I gazed around
Low voices from the scented darkness sang,
In slumbrous human tones :—

Kiss, dream, and die !—love, let thy lips divine
In one long heavenly kiss be seal'd to mine,
      While singing low the flower-crown'd Hours steal by—
Thy beauty warms my blood like wondrous wine—
While yet the sun hangs still in yonder sky,
            Kiss, dream, and die !

Dream,—while I kiss!—Dream, in these happy bowers,
Thy naked limbs and body strewn with flowers,
    Thy being scented thro' with balmy bliss—
Dream, love, of heavenly light and golden showers,
Melting to touch of lips, like this—and this—
    Dream, while I kiss!

Kiss, while I dream!—Kiss with thy clinging lips,
With clasp of hands and thrill of finger-tips,
    With breasts that heave and fall, with eyes that beam—
Long, lingering, as the wild-bee clings and sips,
Deep, as the rose-branch trail'd in the hot stream,—
    Kiss, while I dream!

Kiss, dream, and die!—Love, after life comes Death,
No spirit to rapture reawakeneth
    When once Love's sun hath sunk in yonder sky—
Cling closer, drink my being, drain my breath,—
Soul answering soul, in one last rapturous sigh,
    Kiss, dream, and die!

              As the voice ceased,
There flash'd across the haunted forest-path
A flock so strange that even the happy Maid
Stood still, and gazed. A Spirit led the way
Like Bacchus crown'd with grapes and leaves of
    vine,
And wingéd too like Love; but underneath
The falling tresses of his golden hair

A death's head smiled; on a white steed he rode
Caparison'd with gold; and at his back
The tumult follow'd—Satyrs, Nymphs, and Fauns,
Pale Queens with crowns; dishevell'd naked maids;
Priapus next, the laughing garden-god,
Raining ripe fruit around and leaves of gold;
Then Ethiop dancers, clashing cymbals bright;
And after them, supreme among the rest,
A livid Conqueror like Cæsar's self
With wild beasts chainéd to his chariot-wheels;
Behind him drunken legions blood-bestain'd,
With captives wailing in their midst.   These
    pass'd;
Then, mounted on a jet-black stallion's back,
Herodias, bearing in her naked lap
A hoary, bleeding head; and after her
A troop commingled from all times and climes—
Pale knights in armour, on whose shoulders sat
Nixes or elves; goths, mighty-limb'd and grim;
Pale monks, with hollow cheeks and lean long
    hands;
Nuns from the cloister, whose wild, hectic cheeks
Burn'd red as blood between their ghastly bands;
And bringing up the rear a hideous flock
Of idiot children, twisted with disease,
And laughing in a mad and mindless mirth.

 ·And gazing after them with gentle eyes
The old man sigh'd : 'They follow Death, not
  Love !—
From every corner of the populous earth
They come to mar that primal happiness
Which is the root of being !'

       But I cried,
Raising my hands : 'Is it not pitiful ?
Is it not hateful and most pitiful ?
Lo, out of every innocent bower of flowers,
And out of every bed where Love may sleep,
The Shape with " Thanatos " upon its brow
Dreadfully peeps ! Why may not Man be glad,
Forgetting death and darkness for an hour ?
Is it so evil to be happy ? Nay !
Yet the one cup God proffers to his seed
Is wormwood, wormwood !'

      As I spake the Maid,
Coming upon a little mossy well,
That fill'd up softly as a dewy eye
And ever look'd at heaven through azure tears,
Stood white as any lamb upon the brink,
And on her dim sweet double down below
Dropt leaves and flowers, and smiled for joy to see

Her image broken into flakes of snow
But ever mingling beautiful again
Whene'er the soft shower ceased. While on her
    face,
Serene yet masterful in innocence,
I gazed in awe, the old man answer'd me:
' Ev'n as the Gorgon mother ate her young,
Nature for ever feeds on and consumes
Those creatures who, too frail to quit her breast,
Miss the full height and privilege of Man!
I say again that Man was made supreme,
Radiant and strong, to conquer with a smile
The transports that he shares ;
And he by wisdom or by innocence
May conquer if he will ;
And surely he who learns to conquer Love
Hath learnt to conquer Death! Behold my child!
See where she stands like marble 'mid the beam
That beats so brightly on her sinless brows.
As she is, must thy soul be—if thy soul
Would read our creed aright.'

                        But I return'd,
Bitterly smiling, ' She? thine icicle!
Cold to the kiss of Man, what knoweth she
Of love or joy?'

             Still as a star her face
Turn'd full upon me, with a beam so sad,
So strange in sorrow and divine despair,
My heart within me shook; and though she had
      heard
She spake not, but moved onward silently;
And sinking low his voice, and following her,
Her foster-father cried :
                         'Is there no joy
But riot? Is there no immortal love
To make eternal hunger sweeter far
Than lustful feasts? O blind and wayward one,
Hadst thou but seen what these sad eyes have seen,
The passionate eternal purity
Walking these shadowy woods with silvern feet !
I bear the lifelong glory in my heart,
And with the splendour of its own despair
My soul is glad!'

                    I answer'd him again,
Still mocking, ' Keep thy vision !—she, perchance,
Some night may look on hers !'

                          'By night and day,'
Return'd the Shepherd very solemnly,
' By night and day my child beholdeth him,

And quencheth all the fiery flame o' the sense
Against his image, and is sadly glad.
Perchance ere long thine eyes may see him too,
And kiss his holy feet as she hath done.
But now,' he added, looking sadly down
On the bright bowers around him, ' stay not here ;
For if thou dost, we twain must part, and thou,
Fade back to flower, or dwindle back to beast,
As these thou seest are doing momently.
Come !' And he held me gently with his hand,
And drew me softly on. Like one that sleeps,
And sleeping seems to totter heavy-eyed
Through woods of poppy and rank hellebore,
Feebly I moved ; my head swam ; on my lips
Linger'd sour savours as of dregs of wine,
And all my soul with sick and shameful thirst
Woke, as a drunkard after deep debauch
Wakes to the shiver of a glimmering dawn.
In vain ripe fruits were crush'd against my lips,
In vain the branches with their blossom'd arms
Entwined around me ; vainly in my face
The naked dryad and the wood-nymph laugh'd.
Past these I drave as fiercely as a ship
Before the beating of a bitter wind,
And crushing fruit and blossom under foot,
Tearing the tangled tracery apart,

I wander'd on for hours. Nor did I pause
Till from that wondrous Grove my feet had pass'd,
And once again in open glades we stood
Under the azure canopy of heaven.

Now I beheld we stood upon the bank
Of a broad river flowing along between
Deep banks of flowering ferns and daffodils—
A gentle river winding far away
Under green trees that hung their laden boughs
And shed their fruits upon it lavishly;
Yet cool the water seem'd, and silvern bright
As any star, and on the boughs above it
Sat doves as white as snow, brooding for joy,—
And by its brim one crane of glittering gold
With bright shade lengthening from the pensive
    light
Stood, knee-deep in the mosses of the marge.
Slowly my sense grew clear. 'What place is
    this?'
I murmur'd; 'Say, what place divine is this—
God's home, or Love's, or Death's!' but in mine ear
The gentle voice replied, 'Question no more,
But at the brink stoop down, and bathe thy brows;
And if thou thirstest, drink!' So on the marge
I stoop'd, and in my hollow'd hand did lift

The waters, scattering them upon my face,
And tasting; and the fever from my frame
Fell like an unclean robe, and stretching arms
I, like a man rejoicing in his strength,
Stood calm and new-baptized. Tall by the lake
The old man tower'd, and I beheld his face
Was shining as an angel's, with new light
Of rapture in his eyes; and by his side
The Maid, with lips apart and eager eyes,
Stood bathed in glory of her golden hair
And the great sunlight that encircled her!

Scarce had I drunk, when I was ware of One
Who through the green glades by the river's brim
Walk'd, like a slow star sailing through the clouds
Of twilight; yea the face of him afar
Shone starlike, and around his coming feet
The moon-dew shone. As white and still he seem'd
As some fair form of marble brought to life
And gliding in the glory of a dream;
But from his frame, at every step he took,
Shot light which never yet from marble gleam'd,
And splendour that was never seen in stone.
For raiment, backward from his shoulders blown,
He wore a scarf diaphanous; round his form
A chlamys of the whitest woof of lambs;

But all uncover'd was his golden hair,
His feet unsandall'd. 'Who is this that comes?'
Trembling I cried. But suddenly on his knees
The old man fell, with head submissive bent
In gentle adoration. Then, methought:
'The City of my Dream is close at hand,
And this is He who comes to lead me thither!'
And wonder'd much that while the old man knelt,
The Maid leapt forward with outreaching arms,
And with less fear than hath a yeanling lamb
Feeling its mother on a mead in May,
Thrust out her hand and took his hand who came
And brightening in his brightness led him on
With birdlike cries. Then I perceived her face
Now smiling glorified, and straight I knew
That she was gazing on the lonely love
Of her young soul; that all her maiden dream
Was shining there in substance, fairer far
Than star or flower; that on his face she fed
In palpitating awe, so strange, so deep,
She did not even kiss the holy hand
She held within her own.

'Who comes? who comes?'
I murmured to the old man once again;
'A god—the messenger of gods—his name?

He smileth; mine eyes dazzle in the light
Of his bright smiling!' And the other cried,
Not rising, 'To thy knees! and veil thine eyes,
Lest the ecstatic ray his presence sheds
Blind thee apace! He hath a thousand names,
All sweet; but in these glades his holiest name
Is Eros!' 'Eros!' rapturously I sighed;
And tottering as one drunken in the sun,
Fell at his feet who came; and the pale Maid,
Upleaping in the brightness, fountain-like,
Cried, 'Eros! Eros!' leading Eros on,
While the birds sang and every echo rang.

There was a pause, as when in golden June
The heavens, the glassy waters, and the hills
Throb wrapt in mists of heat as in a dream,
So that the humming of the tiniest gnat
Is heard while in the moted ray it swings,—
There was a pause and silence for a space,
But soon the Shepherd, rising reverently,
Cried: 'Master of these golden groves of Faun,
All hail! Unto thy sacred place I bring
A Pilgrim from the dusty tracts of Time,
A seeker of the secret Beautiful
No ear hath heard; and from the summer bowers,
The gardens, and the glades of vain delight,

Latest he comes, still fever'd from the flush
Of those bright bowers. Him to thy feet I bring,
And if his soul be worthy, thou perchance
Mayst heal his pain!' He ceased; and on the air
There rose the thrill of the divinest voice
That ever on a starry midnight charm'd
The swooning sense of lovers unto dream,—
A voice divine, and in a tongue divine
It spake,—such Greek, such honey'd liquid Greek
As Psyche heard that night beneath the stars
She threw her rose-hung casement open wide
And stood with lamp uplifted, welcoming
Her love, storm-beaten in his saffron veil.
'What seeks he?' ask'd the voice; and lo! I cried,
Uplifting not mine eyes: 'O gentle God,
Surely I seek that City Beautiful
From whence thou comest! Dead I fancied thee,
Fallen with that glorious umbrage of dead gods
Which doth bestrew the forest paths of Greece;
And since thou livest, I can seek no guide
More beautiful than thou!' Whereon again,
Burning like amber in the golden beam,
That nightingale of deities replied,
'O child of man, can the Immortal die?
To love, is to endure; and lo, I am;
But from that City Beautiful thou namest

I come not, and I cannot guide thy steps
Thither, nor further than mine own fair realm.'
Smiling I answer'd, rising to my feet:
' If this thy realm is, Spirit Paramount,
Let me abide within it close to *thee!*
Peace dwelleth here, and Light; and here at last,
As in a crystal mirror, I perceive
The clouds and forms of being stream subdued
Through azure voids of immortality.'

' Come, then,' said Eros, smiling beautiful ;
' And for a season I will lead thy feet,
That thou mayst know my secret realm and me!'
And as he spake he waved his shining hand,
And lo, the cluster'd lilies of the stream
Again were parted by invisible airs,
And through the waters came a shallop slight,
Drawn by white swans that cleft the crystal mere
With webbèd feet as soft as oilèd leaves,
And in the shallop's brow a blood-red star
Burnt wondrous, with its image in the mere
Broken mid ripples into rubied lines.
Slow to the bank it came, and there it paused,
So slight, so small, it seem'd no mortal shape
Might float upon the crystal mere therein;
And Eros pointed, silent, to the boat,

But I, half turning to my grey-hair'd guide,
Question'd with outstretch'd hands and glance of
    eyes,
'And *thou?*'
                    The Shepherd smiled, with gentle hand
Restraining now the Maid, who, stretching arms,
Would fain have follow'd that diviner Form
On whom her eyes were fasten'd, ring in ring
Enlarging, like the iris-eyes of doves.
'Farewell!' he said; 'further I fare not, friend!
For whosoever sails that crystal stream
Must with the golden godhead sail alone.
My path winds homeward, back to the sunny glades
Where first we met. Farewell! a long farewell!
If ever backward through these groves of Faun
Thou comest, seek that Valley where I dwell,
And tell me of thy quest!'
                         Methought I raised
The Maid, and set upon her brow the seal
Of one long kiss; but me she heeded not,
Gazing in fascination deep as Death
On that calm god; then, stooping low, I kiss'd
The Shepherd's hand, and enter'd the bright boat
That on the shallow margin of the river
Did droop the glory of its rubied star
Like some bright water-flower. Beneath my weight

The Groves of Faun.

The shallop trembled, but it bare me up;
And slowly through the shallows lily-sown
It moved, pulsating on the throbbing stream
As white and warm as bosoms of the swans
That drew it. In its wake the godhead swam,
Gold-crown'd; and from beneath the mere his limbs
Gleam'd, like the flashing of a salmon's sides.

Slowly it seem'd to sail, yet swiftly now
The shore receded, till the Man and Maid
Beyond the mists of brightness disappear'd,
And ever till they faded utterly
Moveless the Maiden's face as any star
Shone tremulous with innocent desire,
And when they vanish'd, from the vanish'd shore
There came a quick and solitary cry
That wither'd on the wind.
      Then forth we fared,
Till nought was seen around us or above
But golden glory of the golden Day
Reflected from the bosom of the mere
As from a blinding shield; and, lo! my sense
Grew lost in dizziness and deep delight:
All things I saw as in a dazzling dream,
And drooping o'er them drowsily gazed down
Into the crystal depths whereon I sail'd.

Then was I 'ware that underneath me throbb'd
Strange vistas, dim and wonderful, wherein
The great ghost of the burning sun did shine
Subdued and dim, amid a heaven as blue,
As blue and deep, as that which burnt o'erhead;
And in the under-void like gold-fish gleam'd
Innumerable Spirits of the lake,
Naked, blown hither and thither light as leaves,
With lilies in their hands, their eyes half closed,
Their hair like drifting weeds; thick as the flowers
Above, they floated; near the surface some,
And others far away as films of cloud
In that deep under-heaven; but all their eyes
Were softly upturn'd, as unto some strange star,
To him who in the shallop's glittering wake
Swam 'mid the light of his lone loveliness.

Then all grew dim! I closed my heated eyes,
Like one who on a summer hill lies down
Face upward, blinded by the burning blue,
And in my ears there grew a dreamy hum
Of lark-like song. The heaven above my head,
The heaven below my feet, swam swiftly by,
Till clouds and birds and flowers and water-elves
Were blent to one bright flash of rainbow light
Bewildering the sense. And now I swam

By jewell'd islands smother'd deep in flowers
Glassily mirror'd in the golden river;
And from the isles blue-plumaged warblers humm'd,
Swinging to boughs of purple, yellow, and green,
Their pendent nests of down; and on the banks,
Dim-shaded by the umbrage and the flowers,
Sat naked fauns who fluted to the swans
On pipes of reeds, while in the purple shallows,
Wading knee-deep, listen'd the golden cranes,
And walking upon floating lotus-leaves
The red jacana scream'd.
      Still paramount
Shone Eros, piloting with lily hand
His shallop through the waters wonderful,
And wheresoe'er he went his brightness fell
Celestial, turning all the saffron pools
To crimson and to purple and to gold.
Calm were his eyes and steadfast, with a light
Which in a face of aspect less divine
Would have seem'd sad, and on his brows there lay
A golden shadow of celestial thought.

Thus in my dream I saw him floating on,
While, with dim eyes of rapture downward turn'd,
I feasted on his beauty silently;
And under him the strange abysses swoon'd,

And o'er his head the azure heaven stoop'd down ;
And even as a snow-white steed that runs
Pleased with its burthen, merrily hasting on,
The river rambled on from bank to bank,
In curves of splendour winding serpentine.

Betimes it broaden'd into bright lagoons
Sown with innumerable crimson isles ;
And merrily on the mossy banks there ran,
Pelting each other with ripe fruits and flowers,
Bright troops of naked nymphs and cupidons
With golden bows ; and o'er them in the air
Floated glad butterflies and gleaming doves ;
And ever to the rippling of the river
Rose melody of unseen voices, blown
From the serene abysms far beneath ;
And other voices answer'd from the isles,
And from the banks, and from the snow-white
    clouds
That, flowing with the flowing of the stream,
Trembled and changed, like shapes with lilied hands !

Now one green island stretch'd across the stream,
Paven with purple and with emerald,
And walking there, all wondrous in white robes,
Moved troops of virgins singing solemnly

To lutes of amber and to harps of gold.
Among them, resting on a flowery bank,
Sat one like Bacchus, roses in his hair,
His cheeks most pale with summer melancholy,
Fondling a tigress that with sleepy eyes
Nestled her mottled head into his palm.
O'er head an eagle hover'd with his mate,
And rising slow on great wind-winnowing wings
Faded into the sunset, silently.

Now gazing on these wondrous scenes methought:
' This is enchantment, and these things I see
Only the figures of an antique Joy,
Unreal as shapes in an enchanter's glass
And hollow as a pleasure snatch'd in sleep.'
Suddenly, strangely, answering my thought,
And smiling with a strange excess of light,
Murmur'd that God my Guide : ' Fly from thy
  dream,
And it shall last for ever; cherish it,
And it shall wither in thy cherishing!
These things are phantasies and images
As thou and I are imaged phantasies;
But if the primal joy of Earth is real,
And if thou sharest deep that primal joy,
These phantasies are real—not false, but true.'

Then did I cry, 'If these fair shapes be true,
No dream is false.' And Eros answer'd me:
'All things are true save Sin and Sin's despair,
All lovely thoughts abide imperishable,
Though countless generations pass and die!'

The wonder deepen'd. Earth and Heaven seem'd
    blent
In one still rapture, for their beating hearts
Were prest like breasts of lovers, close together;
And in the love-embrace of Heaven and Earth,
The river, ever-smiling, wound and wound;
And as in beauteous galleries of Art
Picture on picture swooneth past the sense,
Marble with marble mingles mystically,
Till all is one wild rapture of the eyes,
E'en so that pageant on the river's banks
Went drifting by to sound of shawms and songs.
Bright isles with white nymphs cover'd;
    promontories
Whereon immortal nakednesses lay
Singing aloud and playing on amber lutes;
Vistas of woodland, on whose shaven lawns
The satyrs danced with swift alternate feet,
Came, faded, changed; and ever far below
In the dim under-heaven floated fair

Those Spirits singing; and ever far above
Those Spirits slight as flecks of whitest clouds
Still singing floated; and the same still way
The river floated did the heavens move on,
Till all seem'd drawn in a swift drift of dream
To some consummate wonder yet unseen.

And now, the river narrowing once again,
We stole 'neath forest umbrage which o'erhead
Mingled outstretching arms from either bank,
And woven in the green transparent roof
Were glorious creepers like the lian-flower,
And flowers that ran like many-colour'd snakes
Turning and trembling from green bough to bough;
And in the glowing river glass'd with speed
This intertangled golden tracery
Was mirror'd leaf by leaf and flower by flower,
For ever changing and ever flitting past.
Thus gliding, suddenly we floated forth
Upon a broad lagoon as red as blood,
Stainèd with sunset; and no creature stirr'd
Upon or round the water, but on high
A vulture hover'd dwindled to a speck;
And on the shallow marge one silent Shape
Hung like a leafless tree, with hoary head
Dejected o'er the crimson pool beneath;

And no man would have wist that dark Shape
    lived ;—
Till suddenly into the great lagoon
The shallop sail'd, and the white swans that drew it
Were crimson'd, oaring on through crimson pools
And casting purple shadows. Then behold!
That crimson light on him who drave the bark
Fell as the shafts of sunset round a star,
Encircling, touching, but suffusing not
The shining silvern marble of his limbs ;
And that dark Shape that brooded o'er the stream
Stirr'd, lifting up a face miraculous
As of some lonely godhead ! Cold as stone,
Formlessly fair as some upheaven rock
Behung with weary weeds and mosses dark,
That face was ; and the flashing of that face
Was as the breaking of a sad sea-wave,
Desolate, silent, on some lonely shore!

Then Eros as he passed across the pool
Upraised up his shining head, and softly named
Three times the name of 'Pan ;' and that large Shape,
His face upturning sadly to the light,
Reveal'd the peace of two great awful eyes
Made heavenly by the starlight of a smile ;
And as he smiled, the stillness of the place

Was broken, and the notes of nightingales
Fell soft as spray of roseleaves on the air,
And once again the waters far beneath
Were peopled, and the clouds moved on again
In their slow drift of dream they knew not whither;
But Eros swiftly pass'd, and once again
The brooding godhead, sinking in his place,
Hung large and shadowy like a mighty tree
Above the brightness of that still lagoon.

And now methought that far away there rose
Beautiful mountains stain'd with purple shades
And pinnacled with peaks of glittering ice,
And o'er the frosted crystal of the peaks
The trembling splendour of the lover's star
Shone like a sapphire. Thitherward now crept,
Slowly, in bright and many-colour'd curves,
That river, hastening with a living will,
With happy murmurs like a living thing;
And soon it turn'd its soft and flowery steps
Into the bosom of great woods that lay
Under the mountains. Peaceful on its breast
Shadows now fell, while still gnats humm'd, and
    flowers
Closed up their leaves i' the dew; and thro' the
    leaves,

With radiance faintly drawn as spiders' webs,
Trembled the twilight of the lover's star.
At last, against a mossy shore, thick strewn
With violets dewy-eyed, the shallop paused,
And Eros, wading to the grassy bank
Under the shadow of the forest trees,
Cried 'Come!'—and silently I follow'd him
Into the sunless silence of the woods.

BOOK X.

THE AMPHITHEATRE.

AND in my dream, which seem'd no dream at all,
Methought I follow'd my celestial Guide
From path to path, from emerald glade to glade;
And ever as we went, methought the path
Grew with the summer shadows silenter,
While overhead from the great azure folds
Began to stray the peaceful flocks of stars.

Now I perceived before that Spirit's feet
A light like moonlight running, and I heard,
Far away, mystically, in my dream,
The song of deep-embower'd nightingales.
Along the woodland path on either side
There glimmer'd marble hermae crown'd with flowers,
And mid the boughs hung many-colour'd lamps
Like fruit of amber, crimson, purple, and gold.

Last on mine ears there fell a sudden sound
Like shepherds piping or like fountains falling,
A sound that gather'd volume, and became
As music of innumerable harps
And lutes and muffled drums, and therewithal
A heavy distant hum as of a crowd
Of living men together gathering.

Then did I mark that all the forest way
Was thronging unaware with hooded shapes
Who moved in the direction of that sound;
Shadows they seem'd, yet living; and as they went
They to each other spake in quick low tones
And hurried their dark feet as if in haste.
Tall in their midst shone that fair God my Guide,
To whom I whisper'd as we stole along,
'What Shapes are these?' and ' Pilgrims like thyself,'
The Spirit cried; ' but hush, for we are nigh
The midmost of the Shrine.' Ev'n as he spake,
Out of the shadow of the woods we stept,
While on our ears the murmur of the crowd
Grew to low thunder, as of waves that wash
Silent, in darkness, up some ocean strand;
And lo! we saw before us thick as waves
Thousands that gather'd in their pilgrims' weeds

Within a mighty Amphitheatre
Hewn in a hollow of the grassy hills,—
And faces like the foam-fleck'd sides of waves,
Before some wind of wonder blowing there,
Flash'd all one way and multitudinous
Far as the eye could see or ears could hear,
Watching a far-off curtain, on whose folds
Two words in fire were written: 'ΕΡΟΣ. ΑΝΑΓΚΗ.'
More vast that crowded Amphitheatre
Than any hewn in olden time by man,
And round it, and before it, and beyond
That curtain, gather'd crags and monoliths
All rising up to peaks of glittering snow
And in a starry daylight darkening.

Amid that murmur as of sullen seas
Fair Eros moved, and of the shadowy throng
Not one look'd round to gaze, while I and he
Crept to a place, and finding seats of stone
Rested, with eager crowds on either side;
And then I heard a shadow at my back
Murmur some question in an antique speech,
And unto his another voice replied
' Βρότειος '—then the murmur of that throng
Was changed to quick sounds in the same sweet
    speech

Spoken as music by my guide divine,
But as I prick'd mine ears to list for more
There came a solemn silence, and behold,
Suddenly, to a sound of lutes and drums,
The curtain dark descended.
                              Far away,
Upon a sward as green as emerald,
There sat, with wine-gourd lying at his side,
Wild poppies tangled in his hoary hair,
Silenos,—at whose feet a naked nymph
Lay prone with chin propt in her hollow'd hands
Uplooking in his face and reading there
Deep-wrinkled chronicles as soft as sleep;
And overhead among the wild ravines,
On patches of green emerald, leapt his goats,
While far above the sunshine swept like wind
Across the darkness of the untrodden peaks.
To the low music of an unseen choir
Silenos smiling spake, and as he spake
The white goats leapt, the soft light stirr'd
        o'erhead,
The white clouds wander'd through the peaceful blue.
For of much peace he told, of golden fields,
Of shepherds in dim dales Arcadian,
Of gods that gather'd the still stars like sheep
Dawn after dawn to shut them in their folds

And every dawn did loose them once again,
Of vintage and of fruitage, and of Love's
Ripe kisses stolen in the reaping time.
Sweet was his voice, and sweet that mimic scene—
So sweet I could have look'd and heark'd for ever;
And on that sight the throng was hungering,
When suddenly the choral music ceased,
And wearily up the mountains came a wight
Clad like a pilgrim of an antique land.
Tall was he, yet of human height, but there,
Upon that mighty stage, he seemed as small
As pixies be that play in beds of flowers;
And him Silenos greeted, and those twain
Sat on the grassy carpet flower-bestrewn;
And then the stranger told a seaman's tale
Of heroes sailing in their wingèd ships
To flash on Troia like a locust-swarm,
And among those he named his own fair name—
Ulysses.
   Not as in the nether world,
Within some bright and lamp-lit theatre,
The drama calmly moves from scene to scene,
And actors speak their measured cadences
And make their exits and their entrances,
Not thus did that colossal spectacle
Flow on; but as a bright kaleidoscope

Is shaken in the hand, and with no will
Trembles, dissolves, in ever-wondrous change,
The scenes upon that mighty stage did fade,
While the deep voices of the unseen choir
Were rising, falling, all within my dream.
So, even as that grey-hair'd Marinere
Spake with Silenos on the mountain side,
All strangely vanish'd; and before our sight,
To martial music blown through tubes of brass
The Grecian phalanx brighten'd, and afar,
Beyond the Grecian tents as white as snow,
The towers of Ilium crumbling like a cloud
Burnt brazen in the sunset. Suddenly
The shining phalanx and the snow-white tents
Shrunk up like leaves, and in their stead the earth
Was strewn with brightness of a thousand flowers
Mid which a great pavilion lily-white
Bloom'd,—in its centre, seated like a queen,
Helena! Oh, the wonder of that face,
That miracle of lissome loveliness,
That ripe red rose of womanhood supreme!
More fair she seem'd, seen thus from far away,
Than Cytherea rising from the sea
Or seated naked on the lover's star
Strewing the seas beneath her silvern feet
With pearls and emeralds all a summer night!

And from her body and from her breath there came
Waft of rich odours that o'erpower'd the sense,
And all around, strewn thick as fallen leaves,
Were kings and warriors with dishevell'd hair
Kissing her naked feet and with mad eyes
Uplooking in her face!
     Then did I cry:
' O happy Earth, where seed like this is sown,
And grows to such a womanhood divine!
Before the glory of that one fair face
Gods die, gods fade, there is no god but Love!'
And turning, I beheld each face that gazed
Was shining as anointed, for the throng
Was drinking all the sight with rapturous eyes;
But like a marble statue in his place
Stood that pale god my guide—as stone to flesh
His beauty that had seem'd so warm before
Was to that woman's on the mimic stage,
And ever on her face he fix'd his eyes
With hunger of a pity infinite!
There was a silence as of summer seas;
The heart stood still, while brighter and more bright
That glory grew,—till, like a chrysolite,
It dazzled all those upward-looking eyes:
Then slowly, softly, silent as a cloud,
Veiling that miracle of womanhood

The curtain rose.
                    There was a sultry pause,
Such as there comes on summer days of calm,
When every leaf doth seem to hold its breath
And in the golden mirror of the pool
The lily's shadow lies like alabaster.
Each creature in that mighty company
Half closing heavy eyelids, brooded o'er
His own thick heart-beats; only Eros stood
Calm, mute as marble, very fair and pale,
Folding his arms, and on the curtain dark
Reading his own sweet name!
                             Again there came
Vibrations of low music, strangely blown
From out the very hollows of the earth;
These quicken'd, trembled, till there wildly rose
The shrieking sharp of flutes innumerable,
To which once more, curling black folds to earth,
The curtain fell. And lo! on that great stage
Gleam'd Argos, and the statues of the gods
Looming phantasmic in a blood-red moon,
And Clytemnestra on the palace-roof
Uplifting to dark heavens sown sick with stars
A face fix'd white in one avenging spasm
Of murderous pallor; and her stature seem'd
Gigantic, on the high cothurnus raised;

And not a feature of the woman changed,
All kept one horror of the mask they were,
Yea not until afar the beal-fire burn'd
On Ida, did she speak, descending slow,
And like low thunder, from the mask's thick tube,
Her voice was wafted onward to mine ear.
But as she spake that midnight air was cloven
By such a shriek as only once on earth
Was heard by mortal ears.—Cassandra wail'd!

It seem'd as if in answer to that wail
Chaos had come and all the graves of old
Given up their dead; for suddenly the stage
Was cover'd with gigantic shrouded shapes,
Who stood and raised their hands to heaven and
  shriek'd!
And in the dim, low light of blood-red stars
Tower'd Agamemnon bleeding from his wounds;
Iphigenia, like a spectre pale,
Half kneeling, hands uplifted, at his feet;
Orestes, with a dagger in his grip,
Clutching the marble woman, while she shrieked:
' Hold, child! strike not this bosom whence so oft
With toothless gums thy mouth hath drunk the
  milk;'
Eleokles, with fratricidal knife;

Œdipus groping for his daughter's hand,
And white as any lamb that Virgin's self;
And in the background, glaring with cold eyes,
Dumb as a pack of lean and hungry wolves
Full of blood-hunger, the Eumenides!

A wind of horror o'er that gathering grew,
And lo! I shiver'd like a rain-wash'd leaf,
While from the throats of those pale spectres came
Fierce supplications and anathemas
On Zeus, and that pale skeleton that broods
For ever at his footstool, Anarchy.
'God! God!' they shriek'd, and ever as they shriek'd
They gnash'd their teeth and rent their luminous
    robes
And wept anew.   Meseem'd it was a sight
Too much for human vision to endure!
Suddenly, as a black cloud swallowing up
Pale meteors of the midnight, once again
Uprose the curtain.
                   Then in a low voice,
Still shuddering with that horror past, I spake:
'Hear'st thou that cry, which from the dark
    beginning
Pale souls, fate-stricken, have cast up at heaven?
How shall these things have peace?' and in mine ears

'Twas answer'd: 'As the innumerable waves
Sink after tempest to completest calm,
For surcease of the mighty tumult pass'd,
So these wild waifs of being grow subdued
To subtle music of sublime despairs;
For out of wrath comes love, and out of pain
Dumb resignation brooding like a dove
On sunless waters, and of unbelief
Is born a faith more precious and divine
Than e'er blind Ignorance with his mother's milk
Suck'd smiling down! But, hark!' and as he
    spake,
There came a twittering as of birds on boughs,
A music as of rain pattering on leaves;
And to this murmur the great curtain fell,
Revealing slopes of greenest emerald
By shallow rivulets fed with flashing falls,
And far away soft throbb'd the evening star,
And everywhere across those pastures sweet
Moved Lambs as white as snow! Then as I gazed
I heard Apollo singing on the heights
A shepherd's song divine, and as he sang
Those lambs their faces to the light upturn'd,
And each was human: a sweet woman's face,
With large still heavenly eyes wherein there swam
Dews of a dark desire; and lo, I knew

The daughter of Colonos, golden-hair'd,
Electra, still and pensive as a star,
Alcestis pallid from the kiss of Death,
The daughters of Danaos, and the seed
Of Epaphos and Io; and, behold!
Quietly through those mystical green meads
Stole the fair Heifer's self, as white as snow,
Star-vision'd, woman-faced, miraculous,
Come after many wanderings to such peace
As only Love's immortals ever know.
Then down the mountain-sides, a tiger-skin
Back from his shoulders blowing, lute in hand,
As brown as any mortal mountaineer,
Apollo, the glad Shepherd, hastening came,
And cried, ' Rejoice! rejoice! for Zeus is dead!'
And from a thousand throats those lambs did seem
To bleat in human tones, while Io raised
Her moon-like head and utter'd her sad heart
In one rejoicing cry! Then did I turn
My startled eyes on Eros questioning,
And found his face like all those faces round
Was shining as anointed, while his eyes
Were fix'd on that great stage whence thrill'd a voice
Which murmur'd on: ' Rejoice, rejoice, rejoice!
Now shall the sad flocks of Humanity

At last find peace!'
                    In mine own heart of hearts
I echoed, 'Peace!' and that great company
Breathed as a forest's multitudinous leaves
Breathe balmily after rain; but suddenly
That scene kaleidoscopic changed once more,
Came then a thunder as of gathering clouds,
Flashing of torrents down black mountain-sides,
A storm, a troubled darkness, in whose midst
A voice went crying aloud, 'Zeus is!—Zeus reigns!'
And then, the darkness vanishing, behold!
The scene show'd mountains to whose snowy peaks
Fierce cataracts frozen in the act to fall
Clung chain'd in ice,—and in the midst thereof
Gigantic, silent in his agony,
With all the still cold heaven above his head,
Prometheus Purkaieus!
                    Meseem'd he slept:
His eyes were softly closéd, and he smiled
Like one who sleeps yet dreams; and his white hair
Had grown through long eternities of pain
Down to his feet, clothing his limbs like wool,
And the fierce wedge of adamant that pierced
His breast and vitals was with countless years
Rusted blood-red, and hoary all he seem'd
As those ice-ribbèd peaks that hemm'd him round.

Transfixéd were his mighty feet and hands,
As when by Kratos and dark Bias nail'd
To those hard rocks, and brightly yet he bled,
For silently the fountains of his heart
Distill'd their blood like dew !
       Sad was that sight,
And yet I gazed upon it with sweet joy,
For round the head of that great Sufferer,
And on his face, and on his closèd lids,
There brooded peace most absolute and power
Sublimely self-subdued. Afar away
Came voices of the Okeanides,
Singing their sad primæval seabirds' song;
And listening with quick spiritual ears,
Methought I heard, faint as a sound in sleep,
The murmur of these deep eternal seas
Which wash for ever the weary feet of Earth.

Then up those desolate heights, from ledge to ledge
Of living granite, came a godlike shape,
Gigantic, yet smooth-flesh'd and young of limb,
With eagle-eye that faced the midday sun
And shrunk not, leading slowly (as one leads
A wounded horse that falters with its pain),
An aged Centaur,—man from brow to breast,
Bearded and mighty-brow'd and venerable,

But bodied like some grey and mighty steed;
And lo, I knew the first was Herakles,
The second Cheiron; and behold, this last
Was faint thro' one green wound upon his breast,
Deep, bloody, and he stagger'd as he came,
And ofttimes fell upon his quivering knees
And moan'd aloud, beating the solid rock
With hoofs of iron into sparks of fire.

Thereon, I turn'd to Eros questioning:
'Why cometh Cheiron led by Herakles?'
And Eros, on whose face there shone a light
New and ecstatic as the rising moon,
Answer'd: 'Until another immortal god
Contentedly shall take the cup of death,
Taking his stand in that pale Sufferer's place,
Prometheus must abide and drink his doom;
But Cheiron, weary from his wound and weak,
Elects to perish in that pale god's stead,
And hither cometh led by Herakles,
That so the prophecy may be fulfilled.'

And lo, amid the rocks of that ravine,
Face unto face with that pale Sufferer,
Uprose those twain, and slowly at the sound
Prometheus woke, and shaking from his eyes

Eternities of the white blinding hair,
Gazed in their faces dumbly, even as one
Who wakes confusedly and mingles still
That which he sees and that which he hath
    dream'd.
But Herakles cried loud with clarion-voice
' Prometheus !' and the Titan stared and smiled,
Remembering; but as his woeful eyes
Fell upon Cheiron's ghastly lineaments,
He trembled, moaning, ' Who is he that stands
Beside thee, bleeding ?'—and the god replied,
' Cheiron the Centaur, come to take thy place,
To wear thy chains, to suffer, and to die !'

Suddenly, for a moment, that strange scene
Was blotted from the vision, and there rose
A sound as if of many fountains leaping,
Of many wild winds blowing, of many voices
Uplifted in a troublous melody ;
And when the darkness melted, and again
That portent gather'd on the straining sight,
The moon was out and stars serenely bright,
And Herakles had freed Prometheus,—
Who, standing awful in the moonlight, gazed
Around him with a sad and stony stare.
And whiter now he seem'd than any snow,

Clothed in the sorrow of his hoary hairs.
Then, as his chains fell from him with a clang
Of sullen iron, from afar away
There came a cry, ' Prometheus is free—
Rejoice! Rejoice!' and through those wild ravines
From crag to crag, the weary echoes moan'd
' Rejoice!' but pallid still Prometheus stood
Chattering his teeth, while slowly Herakles
Led Cheiron to the rock of sacrifice,
Lifting the chains.
               Even then the dark still air
Was pierced by such a shriek as froze the blood,
Shook reason on her throne and palsied will—
A shriek of eldritch laughter; and, behold!
There suddenly swarm'd in upon that stage
Pigmies innumerable, dragging in
A mighty Cross of blackest ebony!
As swift as thought they set it in the chasm,
Where for eternities of misery
The Titan wail'd, and still they laugh'd aloud,
That the deep chasms of the mountain rung.
Then all the stars shrunk up, and the pale moon
Grew red and shrivell'd, but round Cheiron's brow
Swam suddenly a luminous aureole!
And, lo, his face seem'd changed, and it grew young,
And, as it changed, his nether limbs of beast

Swoon'd into limbs of white humanity,—
And lo, I knew him for that Man Divine
Whose wan face gazeth from the cloudy Book
With wistful eyes! Beneath the mighty Cross,
Crouch'd like a lion couchant hoary-hair'd,
Prometheus waited, while invisible hands
Raised up that other to his place of pain.
Then did the laughter cease, as Herakles
Transfix'd him thro' the shuddering hands and feet,
When dropping chin upon his breast he moan'd,
' My god, my god, hast thou forsaken me?'

Thrill'd thro' the core of that great multitude
A moan of deep insufferable woe!
And I, with heavy hand upon my heart,
Turn'd unto Eros; turning, saw him stand
Transfigured—on *his* hands and on *his* feet
Stigmata red and bloody—round *his* head
An aureole such as that other wore;
And on the Crucified he fix'd his eyes,
And still the Crucified gazed down upon him,
And each was as the image of the other!
Two faces, far asunder, yet the same,
Two faces, one upon that mighty stage,
One in the midst of that vast multitude,
Shone silent, and the moon was white on both!

It was a sight too sad for mortal soul
To look upon and live.   I shriek'd and swoon'd,
And dropt upon the earth as still as stone ;
While all that pageant and that multitude
Pass'd into night as if they had not been !

BOOK XI.

THE VALLEY OF DEAD GODS.

I WOKE: the night had fallen—the scene had changed—
And living yet, I wander'd darkly on.

Alone within a Valley lone as death,
Alone thro' all around me shapes like men
Pass'd wailing, and their crying in mine ears
Was as the waves of ocean when they wash
On sunless arctic shores of rock and ice,
I wander'd, and at every step I took
The shadows of the night grew balefuller;
Yet dimly I discern'd on every side
Black mountains rising up to blacker skies,
And hither and thither forkèd lights that flash'd
O'er gulfs of dread new-riven; and methought
The path I trode was strewn on every side
With tombs of stone and marble sepulchres,
Out of whose darkness look'd the sheeted dead,

Moaning; and oft I paused in act to fall
Into some open grave, and looking down
Saw skulls and bleaching bones and snakelike ghosts
That crawl'd among them.   Then in soul's despair
I call'd aloud on God, and all around
Thunder like hideous laughter answer'd me,
And from the throat of every open grave
Came shrieks and ululation.
                                    Blacker yet
The Valley grew, until in soul's despair
I paused, and, looking upward, saw the heights
Alive with pallid meteors, that like snakes
Crawl'd on the ground, or rose like wan-eyed ghosts
In glimmering shrouds, or plunged into the abyss
And vanish'd; and the wailing all around
Grew thick as clangour of waves that smite each
        other,
Clash back, and smite again; and suddenly
I saw a blood-red star aloft in heaven
Shoot from its sphere, and fall, and after that
Another and another, till all the air
Was luminous and dreadful, sown with drops
Of flame, like blood!   Then, as I upward gazed,
There came a shape in pilgrim's weeds like mine,
Who touch'd my arm and mumbled in mine ear
With voice that seemèd faint and far away:

'They fall! they fall! as thick as leaves they fall,
Unpeopling all the starry thrones of heaven.
Rejoice! rejoice!' And when I question'd him
Of that strange Valley where I walk'd in dread,
He answer'd, laughing feebly in his throat,
'The Valley of the shadows of dead gods!
Rejoice! rejoice! the gods are fallen, are fallen!'

Phantom he seem'd where all was phantom-like,
Yet human. As he spoke, those open graves
Echo'd his cheerless laugh, and the white stones
Chatter'd like teeth, and from the heights a voice
Answer'd, 'Rejoice—the gods are fallen, are fallen!'
Then, pointing with his hand at that red rain
Which ever fell from heaven, 'Behold!' he cried,
'Another and another and another!
Eternity has closed its gates upon them,
Homeless they haunt the void, and fall, and fall!'

Then horror closed upon me like a hand
Clutching mine entrails, while I wander'd on
In darkness visible; and at my back
That greybeard follow'd, wailing, 'Fallen, fallen!'
And presently I saw a sheeted form,
Who sat upon a sepulchre, and struck
A harp of gold and sang: golden his hair,

Above a thin face wasted into bone,
And large regretful eyes; and lo! his limbs
Within the open shroud were wasted not
But beautiful as marble, and his arms
As marble too; and round about him danced
Wild ghosts of naked witches in a ring,
Who sang, 'Apollo! hail, all hail Apollo!'
Then tore their hair and fell upon the ground
And shriek'd aloud; and overhead the clouds
Were riven and sullen peals of thunder shook
The empty thrones of heaven. Shuddering I pass'd,
And came unto a fiery space wherein
Two forms were struggling in a fierce embrace—
One bright and beautiful, one black as night
And wingèd like an eagle; and around
Monsters, like hideous idols wrought in stone,
Yet living, hover'd, uttering shrieks and cries.
And lo! the first, who wore a golden crown
And robes of white and crimson like a king,
O'ercame and would have slain the night-black foe
But that he spread his great wings monster-wise
And shrieking fled!—Pallid with victory,
Yet ring'd around by frantic shapes of fear,
The bright god stood a moment's space and held
A dagger like the sacrificial knife
Up skyward; from the wold wild voices wail'd

His name, the Buddha, while a lightning-flash
Illumed him head to foot in blinding flame,
And underneath his feet the earth was riven,
And lo! he bared his bosom white as snow,
Sheathing the knife therein, and with a moan
Fell prone upon his face,—while those fierce forms
Crept nearer, hovering o'er him where he lay.
Like vultures hovering round a bleeding lamb!

O night of wonder! Thro' that vale accurst
I wander'd, struggling thro' strange seas of souls
That thicken'd on my path like ocean-waves;
And all the place was troubled and alive
With dreadful simulacra of the gods
And ghosts of men; and wheresoe'er I trode
The earth was still torn open into graves.

I saw, methought, on a dark mountain-side
Legions of ghosts that surged and broke to foam
Of waving banners and of hookèd swords
Around a Sepulchre, wherein there sat
One with black eyeballs and a beard of snow,
Who smote his hands together and cried aloud,
' Allah il allah!'—and the crowds around
Echoed the name of Allah, and above
The thunders answer'd Allah, while, behold!

The heavens, blown open high above the peaks,
Reveal'd in bloodiest mirage multitudes
Of phantom armies, struggling, multiplying,
Coming for ever, ever vanishing,
With waving banners and with hookèd swords,
Like those who heard the voice and named the Name
On that dark mountain-side!
                              Then in my dream
I saw the spirits of departed gods
Sweep by like changing forms within the fires
Of Ætna, when the forkèd tongues of flame
Shoot skyward and the lava boils and foams
Down the bright shuddering slopes; so thick and fast
They came and went and changed; and I beheld
Astarté, with her nude dishevell'd train
Of women-worshippers who smote their breasts
And wept and wail'd; Moloch and Baal, two shapes
Inform and monstrous, follow'd by a throng
Of kings in purple and of slaves in rags
And Ethiops clashing cymbals; black-eyed Thor,
Bearded and strong, stript naked to the waist,
Girt round with eager cyclops while he swung
His hammer near the furnace burning red
In a black mountain cavern,—all his face
Gleaming, his form illumed from head to foot
With subterranean fires; Thammuz pale,

Walking through glades of moonlight like a ghost;
Lucifer, serpent-crested, clad in mail,
Shaking his sword at heaven, and with his foot
Set on a writhing dragon: and all I saw
Vanish'd and came again, and vanishing
Gave place to more,—chaos of gods and ghosts
Confusedly appearing and departing;
Every strange shape that Superstition weaves,
That man or fiend hath fashion'd: Gorgons dire,
Chimæras, kobolds, witches, pixies, elves,
Undines, and vampires,—intermix'd with these,
Saints calendar'd and martyr'd; naked nuns
Embraced by satyrs stoled and shaven-crown'd,
Goat-footed; sable-stoled astrologers,
Waited upon by grinning apes and trolds
And wizards waving wands: so that my soul
Was sicken'd and my fever-thicken'd blood
Paused in me and surcharged my fearful heart
Until it ceased to beat: and as I fled
Weeping, all faded like a tempest-cloud,
And lonely in the night before my face
I saw the form of the eternal Sphynx
Dreadfully brooding with cold pitiless eyes
Fix'd upon mine, and round it momently
Sheet-lightning play'd, and 'tween its stony claws
It held a woman's naked bleeding corpse

From which the shroud had fallen, and from its
    throat
There came a murmur like the whole world's
    moan,
Thunder of doom and uttermost despair!

Frozen to stone, I stood and gazed and gazed,
Dead-eyed as that vast Shape!
                      The Vision pass'd
Like vapour from a mirror. Night again,
With one black wing of tempest, blotted out
That portent; and before my face I saw
A pale god with a dove upon his wrist,
Sitting upon a tomb and singing low
Some strange sweet song of summer; then, with
    tears,
He named the name of his fair brother Christ,
And search'd the gloom with bright blue heavenly
    eyes,
And listen'd for a coming; and methought
I heard a sound of wailing, and, behold!
Along the valley came three woman-forms
Supporting One who seemèd sick and spent,
A crown of thorns upon his bleeding brow,
Blood-drops upon his piercèd feet and hands,
And in his dexter hand a lanthorn-light

That flicker'd in the wind; and as they came,
These women wail'd aloud, 'He hath arisen!'
And joyfully his blue-eyed brother rose
To greet him coming, but shrank back beholding
The thin grey hair, the worn and weary cheeks,
The pale lacklustre orbs of him who came
Unwitting whither,—wearied out and spent
With centuries of sorrow and despair.

But Balder cried, uplooking in his face,
'O brother, hast thou risen?' and that other,
Moving his head feebly from side to side,
And groping with his hands, moan'd, 'Risen!
    risen!'
Like one who dying murmurs to himself
Some echo from the weepers who surround
His piteous bed of doom; and as he spake,
His eyes grew dimmer, and his bearded chin
Fell forward on his breast, and like a corpse
He swung upheld by those wan women who wail'd
'Rejoice! for Christ hath risen!'
                            Then methought,
While Heaven and Hell moan'd answer to each
    other,
And throngs of gods like wolves around a fire
Gather'd, and earth as far as eye could see

Was one wild sea of open graves, that broke
To foam of dead shapes shining in their shrouds,
I heard a voice out of the darkness calling
And weary voices answering as it sang :—

> Black is the night, but blacker my despair;
> The world is dark—I walk I know not where;
>   Yet phantoms beckon still, and I pursue—
> Phantoms, still phantoms! there they loom—and there!
>   Adonai! Lord! art thou a Phantom, too?
>
> One strikes—before the blow I bend full weak;
> One beckoning smiles, but fades in act to speak;
>   One with a clammy touch doth chill me thro'—
> See! they join hands in circle, while I shriek,
>   Adonai! Lord! art thou a Phantom, too?
>
> Dark and gigantic, one, with crimson hands
> Upstretch'd in protestation, frowning stands,
>   While tears like blood his night-black cheeks bedew—
> He tears his hair, he sinks in shifting sands—
>   Adonai! Lord! art thou a Phantom, too?
>
> The sad, the glad, the hideous, and the bright,
> The kings of darkness, and the lords of light,
>   The shapes I loved, the forms whose wrath I flew,
> Now wail together in eternal night—
>   Adonai! Lord! art thou a Phantom, too?

Fall'n from their spheres, subdued and overthrown,
Yet living yet, they make their ceaseless moan,
   Where never grass waves green or skies are blue—
Theirs is the realm of shades, the sunless zone,
   Where thou, O Master, weeping wanderest too!

O Master, is it thou thy servant sees,
Cast down and conquer'd, smitten to thy knees?
   Ah, woe! for thou wast fair when life was new—
Adonai! Lord! and art thou even as these?
   A shape forlorn and lost, a Phantom too?

Black is the night, but blacker my despair;
The world is dark—I walk I know not where;
   Yet phantoms beckon still, and I pursue!
Phantoms, still phantoms! there they loom—and there!
   Adonai! Lord! art thou a Phantom, too?

And while the voices wail'd, I watch'd his face
Who swung in anguish to and fro, upheld
By those wan women; and the face was blank
And bloodless, his eyes sightless, and his jaw
Hung heavy as lead; and still the women cried
'Rejoice! for He hath risen!' but when at last
The music of those voices died away,
He slipt from their thin hands and with a spasm
Shot forward on his face and lay as dead,
Still as a stone, while all the mighty vale

The Valley of Dead Gods.

Was shaken as by earthquake, and afar
The solid night-black heavens were riven as rocks,
And thunder answer'd thunder!
      Then the waves
Of darkness breaking on me like a sea
Seem'd to o'erwhelm me, and I sank and sank
Down, down to unknown depths of black despair,
Till sense and feeling fail'd me and methought
The end of all was come; but when again
Life flow'd within me, I was wandering still
In that sad Valley; and all forms and shapes
Had vanish'd, and the place was sleeping calm
Under a piteous moonlight. Overhead
The ebon peaks touch'd the cold heavens, alive
With stars like feeble specks of silver sand,
And all the heavens and the sad space beneath
Were silent as a sepulchre!
      Forlorn
And broken-hearted, then I wander'd on,
With tombs and open graves on either side,
Weeping nor wailing, but subdued to calm
Of weariest despair; and no thing stirr'd
Around me, but full tide of silence fill'd
The shoreless earth and heaven; when suddenly
I saw before me, lying on the path,
One like myself in dreary pilgrim's weeds,

Fall'n prone upon his face; and stooping down,
I turn'd his wan face upward to the light,
And knew him,—Faith, my townsman, cold and dead!
His blind eyes glazèd with the frosty film,
Cold icicles in his white hair and beard,
His right hand gripping still the empty leash
Which once had held his beauteous snow-white hound,
Now fled for ever to some sunless cave
To wail in desolation. Then my force
Fell from me, and my miserable eyes
Shed tears like blood, and, broken utterly,
I took the poor grey head between my knees,
Making a pillow, and with gentle hand
Smoothing the piteous hair, murmur'd aloud
A sad song sung by women in our town
While weaving long white raiment for the dead,
When the corpse-candles burn and all the night
Time throbs the minutes like a beating heart
To those who weep and wait.
                                   And thus I sang:—

>   Dead man, clammy cold and white,
>   With thy twain hands clench'd so tight,
>   With thy red heart and thy brain
>   Silent in surcease of pain,
>   Wherefore still in strange surprise
>   Fix thine eyes?

Glass'd to mirror some strange ray
Gleaming ghostwise in the day,
Staring silent, in amaze,
Dead man, glimmereth thy gaze,
Glazing through thy cold grey hair
    With sick stare.

Not on men, and not on me,
Not on aught the living see,
Gazest thou—but still, alas!
Thou perceivest something pass
I perceive not, tho' its thrill
    Cometh chill.

Dead man, dead man, take repose!
Since thy twain eyes will not close,
I will shut them softly over
With the waxen lids for cover;
Look no more upon the sun—
    All is done!

And singing thus I knew (within my dream)
That all the gods were dead, and Death was King,
For all the woeful Valley once again
Grew populous with silent ghostly shapes
Tumultuously moving, like a sea;
And gazing thro' my tears I saw, within
The heart of that black valley, a Form that rose
Gigantic, crag-like, frosted o'er and o'er

With the cold crystals of eternity,
Yet naked as a skeleton; and, lo!
I knew the shape and lineaments of Death,
Lord of the gods and chaos, first and last
Of portents and of phantoms: huge he rose,
Swarm'd on by that tumultuous tide of ghosts
Which broke around his feet; and round him stretch'd
The realm of tears and silence, and above him
Heaven open'd,—an abyss of nothingness
Far as Despair could see or Hope could wing!

BOOK XII.

THE INCONCEIVABLE.

SADDER than night, and sunless as the grave,
   Was that strange darkness clouding soul and
      sense ;
But when I saw the living light again,
And felt the blood within me crawling cold
As drops of quicksilver from vein to vein,
I stood alone upon a wan wayside
Watching the crimson eyeballs of the Dawn.

Darnels and nettles gather'd bosom-deep
Around a rain-worn Cross whereon there clung
No shape of flesh or stone, but from beneath
Came a white glimmer as of bleaching bones ;
And on the Cross a lonely raven sat
Preening his ragged plumage silently ;
And all around were bare and leafless woods
Through which the sunshafts straggled crimson
      red ;
And crouching in the shadow of the Cross

Three spectral Women wrapt in ragged weeds
Sat moaning; and of these the first was old,
With hair as white as wool blown loose and wild
Around her; and the second woman bare
A lighter load of years, with jet-black hair
Just touch'd with hoarfrost; but the third was young,
With eyes of pallid speedwell-blue, and hair
Pure golden raining round her ripe round arms
And naked breasts. And unto these I spake,
Remembering that beauteous god, my guide,
And question'd them of Eros, if their eyes
Had seen him pass that way along the woods
Quitting the woeful Valley of dead gods?

And one said: 'He who suckled at my breast
Is dead and cold, and walks the world no more;'
The second said: 'The vineyard is destroyed;
The Master of the vineyard sleeps for ever;'
And the third said: 'He whom I loved, whose feet
I wash'd and then anointed, at whose tomb
I have knock'd aloud for countless weary years,
Is dead, and hath not risen;' and all the three
Lifted their voices wailing piteously.

Ev'n as I look'd and listen'd woe-begone
I heard a voice behind me murmuring

'Good morrow;' and quickly turning I beheld
A gentle wight, who wore around his form
A pleasant woodland robe of grassy green,
Brown shoon upon his feet, and in his hand
Carried a staff enwound with ferns and flowers;
And when I question'd 'Who are these who weep?'
Upon those women wailing 'neath the cross
He gazed in pity, not in pain like mine,
And answer'd,—
   'Outcasts from the world. Poor leaves!
Fall'n with the rain that beats upon a grave.'

The Pilgrim.

Methinks I know them. Yesternight I saw
These shadows, 'mong the shadows of dead gods.

The Man.

Comest thou from thence? Well may thy cheek
  be pale,
Thy look wayworn and desolate, thy soul
Haunted and woeful. Hast thou wander'd far?

The Pilgrim.

Yea, thither and hither, from Christopolis.

THE MAN.

And whither goest thou? From the darkness
    yonder,
Surely to some new sunshine? Comfort, friend !
The wailing of these wanderers cannot drown
The music of the mountains and the streams,
And scarce a stone's-throw from this piteous
    place
The sunshine falls on crystal rivulets
And warms the snowy fleece of leaping lambs !

Clear was his voice, yet dreamy-toned and deep
As is the wood-dove's cooing when it broods
On its warm heartbeats; and his face, though
    grave,
Was brown as ripen'd fruit and wore no shade
Of fear or sorrow; and even as he spake
The morning brighten'd, and from far away
The silver clarion of the Spring was blown
To wake the drowsy world. 'Alas !' I cried,
'How shall the sunshine and the dawn avail,
Since the sweet gods that made creation glad
Are flown, and Eros, sweetest and most blest,
Bends weeping o'er his Brethren slain and cold
In yonder Valley of Divine Despair?'

The Man.

Take comfort.   Though the many pass away,
The One abides; God bends o'er these dead gods,
And smiles them into everlasting sleep.

The Pilgrim.

Sleep?   But they sleep not!   Weary ghosts, they haunt
That Valley, and the ears of weary men
Can hear them wailing from the gates of Death;
And lo, without their open sepulchres,
In every land beneath the sun and stars,
Women like these prolong and echo back
The piteous ululation.   Woe is me!
Where shall I find a place on all the earth
That is not haunted and disconsolate?

The Man.

Walk these green woods with me, and thou shalt hear
The merry music of the waking world!

The Pilgrim.

What is thy name, and wherefore, dwelling here,
So close to that dread Valley, canst thou keep
A mien so peaceful and a voice so calm?

THE MAN.

Sylvan they name me, after some brave god
Who found my mother sleeping in the shade,
Naked and warm and drowsy from her bath
In a great slumberous pool, and in his arms
Clasp'd her before she woke and quicken'd in her
A newer life, mine own; and when I lived
And drank the light, she told me with a smile
That she had never seen my father's face,
Yet knew by many a sign of leaf and flower
Some godhead had embraced her as she slept!

THE PILGRIM.

Didst thou not say but now, the gods were dead?

SYLVAN.

The gods of sorrow, but the gods of joy
Ever abide where'er the woods are green
And sunlight merry. Every flower and tree
Shares light and life with them, and is divine.

THE PILGRIM.

A phantasy! With such a phantasy
They sought to cheat me in the groves of Faun.

Sylvan.

The many pass away, but Pan abides,
And him we worship in these peaceful woods.

Now, as he spake, those forms beneath the Cross
Grew fainter, and their dreary voices ceased.
Creeping from underneath with scented arms
A honeysuckle and a rose-tree twined
Their tendrils round the Cross, and overspread it
With tender bells and blooms; and as I gazed
Meseem'd they lived and laugh'd to feel the life
Sparkling within them, while their scented breath
Perfumed the air I drew; while all around,
As at the touch of a magician's wand,
The woodland kindled into emerald flame,
The grass along the sward ran bright and green,
O'erhead the morning skies broke bright and blue,
And the great sun became the golden heart
Of the violet of heaven. And Sylvan said:
' Yea, verily the many gods are dead,
Yet that which was their life and quicken'd them
Breaks into summer blossom o'er their graves.'
Whereon I answer'd, walking sadly on
Beside him down the gladdening greenwood glade.

'Christopolis remains, and in its core
Death sits, a crimson King; and hitherward,
And yonder far as the wide gates of dawn,
His sceptre rules both gods and thinking things
As well as tree and flower; and high as heaven,
He sets as sign of his sad sovereignty
The empty Cross!' But Sylvan, smiling, said:
'Death is the servant of the One we serve,
Whose breathing fills the world with light and life.'

The Pilgrim.

Name me his name, that I may understand.

Sylvan.

Nameless and formless is that Life Divine.

The Pilgrim.

Hast thou not known him with thine eyes and ears?

Sylvan.

He dwells for evermore but dimly guessed.

The Pilgrim.

A riddle, like the riddle of the Cross!

Sylvan.

A certitude, like thine own beating heart!
The Ever-changing yet Unchangeable
Haunts His creation as the breath within
Thy body, and as the blood within thy veins:
Moves in the mountains, fills the surging seas,
Melts in the storm-cloud and becomes the dew
That dims the lover's eyes.

The Pilgrim.

                    Meseems I read
Thine easy riddle. He thou worshippest
Is shapeless as the blue ethereal air;
Not God who builds a City for his own,
But that blind force whereby all cities fall?

Sylvan.

What He destroys he evermore renews,—
As He renews the flowers and forest-trees.

The Pilgrim.

Can he renew this desolate heart of dust
Failing away within me as the seed
That rots and falls away within the shell?

Can he roll back the sun and summon back
The boy who gladden'd in the morning time?
Can he bring back the gods whom he has slain,
Sweetest and best the god of flesh and blood
For whom those three wan women weep and wail?

SYLVAN.

He can do more. With every dawn of day
He recreates—

THE PILGRIM.

The mirage of a world!
O peace, for he thou fondly worshippest
Is not the God I seek, but him I fly.

We wander'd on, and all around us grew
Full sweetness of the summer. Green and glad
The prospects brighten'd round us, and I saw
Beyond the emerald reaches of the glade
A leafy valley, meadows, groves, and streams,
With fountains sparkling and upleaping lambs;
And here and there a lonely human form
Flitted across the sunlight and was gone;
Yet for the rest the place was solitary
And full of strange and solitary sounds—

The wood-dove's brooding call, the whispering rill
Half drown'd in rustling leaves, the lambkin's cry
Distant and drowsy, and from time to time
A far-off human call.   Upon my heart
Fell a warm heaviness and dreamy sense
Of happiness fantastic and unreal,
When, looking back, I saw along the glade
Those three wan Women slowly following
In silence, and the pathway as they came
Was sunless, dark, and chill.   'Alas!' I said,
'This valley where you dwell is haunted, too,
By the dim ghosts of goddesses and gods;'
And as I spake we left the woods behind
And came 'mong grassy slopes that wander'd on
To pastoral mountains green and beautiful
Crown'd by the golden noontide.   Here I paused
And pointing upward cried, 'What land lies yonder?'
And Sylvan said, 'A beauteous mountain land
Of Shepherds; but at every height you climb
The air grows chillier, till beneath your feet
Crumble the stainless crystals of the snow.
Be warn'd and fare no further.   Rest content
Here in the lap of summer, laden ever
With roses of the dawn.'
      And as he spake
The sunlight brighten'd, and the leaping lambs

Cried faintly, and the cuckoo call'd her name,
Deep hidden in the sunlight's golden cage;
And round my feet the warm grass crept like moss,
Warm, green, and living, and the golden glades
Kindled and blossom'd,—yet afar away
Behind me still I saw those three wan Shapes
Outlooking from the greenness of the woods.

'Stay!' cried he, as I faced the steep ascent
And hasten'd heavenward; but, mine eager heart
Fill'd with the summer as a cup with wine,
Renew'd and strong, I left him standing there
'Mong those bright pastures; and as sings a lark
For bliss of the glad beating of the wings
That waft it upward, so methought my soul
Ran over gladly, and 'twas thus I sang:—

>   Hark, I am call'd away!
>   Fain would my spirit stay,
>   Here, where the cuckoos call,
>   Here, where the fountains play
>   From dawn to evenfall,
>   Here, where the white flocks stray,
>   With the blue sky spanning all!
>   Here, where the world is May,
>   Fain would I rest, grow grey,—
>   But nay, ah nay!

The Inconceivable.

Birds on the greenwood spray
Flit through the green and the grey,
Flocks on the green slopes cry,
Softly the streams glance by,
All things are merry and gay
Under the morning sky;
Sweet smiles the world to-day,
Yet must I wander away?
    Ah yea, ah yea!

A motion all things obey,
A breath in the cloud and the clay,
A stir in the fountain that springs,
A sound in the bird that sings,
From dawn to death of day
Quick in the heart of things!
All changes, and naught can stay;
Blown like a breath o' the spray,
    I must away!

Ah, would that I could stay!
Yet, as those clouds obey
Winds that behind them blow
(See them, how soft, how slow,
Thro' the still heavens they stray!),
Onward I too must go!
No space to pause, to pray,
But heavenward, even as they,
    I must away!

And now methought I came into that land
Of pastoral mountains, with green summer cones,
Forests of pine and fir upon their flanks,
And waterfalls that flashing silver feet
Leapt with wild laughter into dark ravines;
A land of sheep and shepherds; o'er the slopes
The snow-white flocks were spilt like broken streams,
While faintly overhead against the blue
Sounded a shepherd's horn. In sooth, it seem'd
A green, a peaceful, and a pleasant land!

Climbing the shoulder of a sunlit hill,
Oft gazing back on him I had left behind
Dwindled by distance to a pigmy's size,
I reach'd a solitary cottage door,
And there a mountain maid with gentle eyes
Gave me sweet welcome, placed me in the porch,
And brought me mountain cheer—brown bread and
    milk.
Around my seat flock'd children flaxen-hair'd,
Brown men, barefooted maids, and wise-eyed dogs;
And when I question'd of that peaceful land,
And of the City throned in solitude
Somewhere amid the silence of the hills,
They look'd at one another wondering
And could not understand. But one, a wight,

Grey-hair'd yet lithe, in goatskin mantle clad,
Said: 'Master, I have wander'd, man and boy,
These hills for seventy years, and seen no City,
Save only cities in the sunset clouds
Or in the mirage of the rainbow'd heights:
Be warn'd by me,—turn back, or rest thee here;
The crags are perilous without a guide.'
I answer'd: 'God my Guide and Shepherd is;
I need no other;' and I took my staff,
And bidding them farewell, I hasten'd on;
And as I climb'd the hill look'd back once more
And saw them cluster'd—children, men, and maids—
Watching me as I wander'd up the heights.

Then, faring onward towards the mountain-tops,
I saw a herdboy like an antique Faun
Sitting upon a knoll, and piping sweet,
While round about him leapt his yeanling lambs
And gentle mountain echoes answer'd him.
Bare was his neck and brown, his cheek more red
Than are the berries of the mountain ash,
His hair like golden flax, his voice as clear
As cuckoos crying round the lake-lilies
That open'd on the mountain mere close by.
Him for a little space I gazed upon,
Then greeted with a smile and question'd him,

Singing my question from a merry heart,
Till, smiling too and singing, he replied:—

THE PILGRIM.

Little Herdboy, sitting there,
With the sunshine on thy hair,
And thy flocks so white and still
Spilt around thee on the hill,
Tell me true, in thy sweet speech,
Of the City I would reach.

'Tis a City of God's Light
Most imperishably bright,
And its gates are golden all,—
And at dawn and evenfall
They grow ruby-bright and blest
To the east and to the west.

Here, among the hills it lies,
Like a lamb with lustrous eyes
Lying at the Shepherd's feet;
And the breath of it is sweet,
As it rises from the sward
To the nostrils of the Lord!

Little Herdboy, tell me right,
Hast thou seen it from thy height?
For it lieth up this way,
And at dawn or death of day
Thou hast surely seen it shine
With the light that is divine?

The Little Herdboy.

Where the buttercups so sweet
Dust with gold my naked feet,
Where the grass grows green and long,
Sit I here and sing my song,
And the brown bird cries 'Cuckoo'
Under skies for ever blue!

Now and then, while I sing loud,
Flits a little fleecy cloud,
And uplooking I behold
How it turns to rain of gold,
Falling lightly, while around
Comes the stir of its soft sound!

Bright above and dim below
Is the many-colour'd Bow;
'Tis the only light I mark,
Till the mountain-tops grow dark,
And uplooking I espy
Shining glow-worms in the sky;

Then I hear the runlet's call,
And the voice o' the waterfall
Growing louder, and 'tis cold
As I guide my flocks to fold;
But no City, great or small,
Have I ever seen at all!

So, sighing deep, I pass'd upon my way,
Not strengthen'd, but more spiritually calm

Because the little herdboy's voice was sweet;
And now my pathway by a streamlet ran,
And in the midst upon a mossy stone
Sat the white-breasted ouzel of the brook,
Plunging with soft chirp ever and anon
Into the crystal pool beneath her feet,
And rising dripping dewily to her throne
In the mid stream; and at the streamlet's brink
A lamb stood drinking, and I saw beneath
The stainless shadow broken tremulously
'Mid troubled shallows into flakes of snow.

Then, journeying ever upward, I beheld
The crags and rocks and air-hung precipices
Redden in sunset, and above the peaks,
Upon a bed of crimson duskly gleam'd
The argent sickle of the beamless morn;
And lo, the winds had fallen and curl'd themselves
Like tired-out hounds in hollows of the hills,
Restlessly sleeping but from time to time
Audibly breathing; and deep stillness lay
Upon the mountains and the darkening slopes
Beneath their snows, and the low far-off moan
Of torrents deepening that stillness came
From the untrodden heights.
       Hung like a shield

Midway between the valley and the peaks
There lay a lone and melancholy mere;
And in its glass the hills beheld themselves
Misting the image with their vaporous breath.
Hither, while yet the sunset lit the crags,
Mirror'd below tho' it had faded long
From the dark hollows and the mere itself,
I came, and sitting on its margin watch'd
The faint light fade below me, softly changing
From pink to crimson, and from crimson dark
To darker purple, while one quiet star
Crawl'd like a shining insect of the depths
Upon the azure bottom of the mere.
Ev'n as I sat and mused I heard a voice
Behind me. Quickly turning I perceived
A gray grave mortal like a mountaineer
With crook and leathern shoon, his stature tall,
His shoulders stooping, and his eyes cast down
As if to read a book upon the ground;
Who gently greeted me, and courteously,
Like one mild-vestured in authority,
Welcomed me to that solitary place.

'What man art thou?' I ask'd. 'A friend,' he said,
'To all who cross this way on pilgrimage.
My name is Peaceful, call'd by simple folk

The Hermit of the Mere.'
                              'A lonely place,'
I answer'd; 'lonely, yet most beautiful!
Its calm and loveliness are on thy brow,
Its music in thy voice which sounds to me
Soft as a fountain falling.   Hast thou found
Here, up among the hills, the Gate wherein
The pearl which passeth understanding lies,
And which for evermore with restless feet
We world-worn pilgrims seek?'
                                Upon my face
Fixing the untroubled splendour of his eyes,
'Be comforted,' he said, 'for thou hast reach'd
Those heights where the Seraphic Shepherd guides
The world's sad flocks to their eternal fold;
Thou seekest God.   His stainless Temple stands
Among these mountains!'

                    THE PILGRIM.
                         Dwelling here alone,
Hast thou beheld Him with thy living eyes?

                    PEACEFUL.
I have beheld the flowers o' the earth and sky,
The stately clouds that march and countermarch,
The shining spheres; these evermore fulfil

His ministrations; radiant is the Light
That covers up his face as with a veil;
Soft is the shadow He in stooping casts
Nightly to bless the still and sleeping world!

The Pilgrim.

The God I seek is not so solitary;
He hath built a City for His worshippers!

Peaceful.

Nay, friend; for he who seeks the living God
Must seek Him in the gentle solitude.
Here doth His presence brood in peace for ever
Still as the silence on the mountain-tops;
And he who findeth it, as I have found,
Must leave the flocks of men, and dwell alone.

Ev'n as he spake, and hush'd in awe I shrank
As one that shrinks and dreads the sudden birth
Of some miraculous divine event,
There pass'd across the scene we gazed upon
A mist like sudden breath: cloud follow'd cloud,
And underneath the mountains and the mere
Blacken'd, till utter darkness of the night
Enwrapt us fold on fold; when, suddenly,

s

Out of the vapour rolling down the peaks
Red lightning came, before whose glaring spear
The Thunder, like a wounded monster, crouch'd
And shook with echoing groans!
                          And with that change
My spirit changed within me, from deep dread
Back to familiar trouble and unrest;
But as I stood and wonder'd, hesitating,
Methought that grave and gentle mountaineer
Did lead me to the shelter of his hut
Built by the lonely mere; and there we sat
Together, while the tempest crash'd without
And rain made leaden music on the roof;
A flickering lamp of oil our only light,
Which served to show the peace upon his face,
The unrest on mine; when, marvelling much to
    mark
His mien of gentleness and happiness,
I brake the silence, thus :—
                             'Aye me! methinks
There is no resting-place or succour here
Among these mountains! Needless 'twere to
    climb
So high to find the calm and storm of God.
But 'tis the promised City that I seek—
A City of clear sunlight and sweet air,

Not darkness, and a mystery, and a change,
Fretting the spirit with primæval fear.'

'O friend,' he answer'd, 'I who speak have found
Peace passing understanding in my home
In this great solitude. What seek'st thou more?
Is 't not enough to feel for evermore
The present of the fair Artificer
Who made the holy heavens and the earth
And all within them? Can His living breath
Not still thee, but thou criest for a sign?'

Thereon I rose, and striding to the door,
Look'd forth into the night; and, lo, the storm
Had pass'd away, leaving that mountain air
The calmer for its coming—the blue void
Was sown with stars like snowdrops; on the mere,
Filmy with mist and moonlight, luminously
Like living things their bright reflections stirr'd;
And all the pathos and the peace of heaven
Was pour'd upon the world in pensive beams.

Then rising too the hermit join'd me there,
And, looking upward with me, gently said:
'Still is the night and peaceful once again.
Have patience—so shalt *thou*, too, lie and bask

Under the beams of God. Come in and rest;
To-morrow, if thou wilt, fare forth again,
But be my guest this night!'
       He led me in,
And on the hearth he strew'd a simple bed
Of rushes dry and sweetly-scented fern,
Whereon I sighing threw my wearied limbs,
And for a time I toss'd in dark unrest,
But slept at last; and when I open'd eyes
The merry light was flooding all the place,
And mountain, mere, and torrent were rejoicing
In the new dawn of day.
      Then in the hut
We twain broke bread together and join'd hands
In fellowship of love; but when he sought
To urge me to remain in that still land,
A hermit like himself, I seized my staff
And pointed to the mountain-tops that flash'd
Their kindled peaks above us.
       'Yonder lies
The path that I must follow, though it lead
To utter darkness and to death,' I cried.
'Nor deem my soul ungrateful for this help
Wherewith, most gentle and benign of friends,
Thou hast sought to cheer my spectre-troubled way.
But what thou dreamest I can never dream

By these still waters; what thou dost behold
I, haunted out of patience, out of peace,
By that wild mirage of a heavenly City,
I, faint from a dark Valley of dead gods,
Behold not; what thou findest mirror'd brightly
Within thee as within that gentle mere,
Alas, I cannot find, being darken'd ever
And clouded with a fear: wherefore our ways
Part gently, and my lips must say farewell.'

'So be it,' he answer'd. 'As the bow was bent
The dart must speed; pray Heaven thy soul at last
May hit its lonely mark! But since thy path
Is upward; I will guide thee for a space
Through yonder desolate and dark ravines.
High up among them, under shadowy crags,
One who once wander'd in the sun with me,
Nightshade by name, a lonely mountaineer,
Hath of a rocky cavern made his home.
He knows the loneliest summits and the heights
Familiar with the morning, and perchance
May help thy footsteps onward, where the peaks
Grow steep and perilous!'
                              So side by side
We wander'd on together till we past
From sunlight to the shadow of the hills;

And as we went he spake in stately speech
Of pleasures that made glad his hermitage—
Of moonrise and the wonders of the mere,
Of flowers and stars, white lambs, and lamb-like men;
So that I linger'd listening to his words,
And oftentimes glanced back with doubting eyes
On the bright waters and his happy home.

But now the clarion of the winds was blown
From height to height, and far above our heads
A sunbeam, springing godlike on a crag,
Stood tremulous, pausing between earth and heaven;
And my feet hasten'd, and I felt once more
The motion of the life within my veins
Drifting with wind and light and mist and cloud.
Dark was the way, my path a torrent's bed
Dried up to spots of dusty quicksilver
And strewn with fallen rocks; but eagerly
I hasten'd, till at last my gentle guide
Paused, pointing, and I saw beneath a rock
One Nightshade sitting with lacklustre eyes
Gazing upon the ground and counting thoughts
Like one who telleth beads.
     And for a space
He saw us not, though standing near his seat
We watched him; but at last, like one that wakes

Out of a heavy sleep, he turn'd his head,
Saw us, and welcomed with a dreamful smile.
Him Peaceful greeted, and deliver'd forth
My name and errand,—when that other rose,
Grasping my outstretch'd hand in both of his,
And peer'd into my face like one that reads
A dark and mystic book.
     'Pilgrim of God,'
He murmur'd, 'welcome to these lonely crags,
Wherein, with mystic sounds of death and birth,
The chaos of the Elemental stirs
To Thought ineffable!'
     Even as he spake
He seem'd to fall again into a trance,
Whereon the other gently smiling said,
'Go with him! even as the swift izzard,
Which safely walks the sword-edge of the cliffs,
Or as some angel-led somnambulist
Who falters not where waking men would fall,
He knows the paths of peril.'
     Then once more
We two wrung hands and blessing one another
Parted. And lightly downward Peaceful ran
Until he left the shade of the ravine
And stood in golden sunlight far away
Uplooking, waved his hand, and from my sight

Vanish'd for ever.
                    Then to the other turning,
I told him of my quest and soul's desire
For certainty and peace; 'But surely now,'
I added, 'surely now the end is near,
And I shall share the heavenly sight which fills
Thy face with rapture of mysterious dream!'
He answer'd not, but, muttering to himself,
Walk'd upward, choosing a dark path which seem'd
To wander right into the stony heart
Of those wild mountains: soon the riven rocks
Rose o'er us, leaving only one blue space,
A hand's breadth wide, to show the open heaven;
And as one lying in an empty well
May, though full daylight burns beyond it, see
Stars circling in their orbits, I beheld
On that blue patch of space above my head
The gleam of constellations. Darker yet
The pathway grew, and now on every side
Gulfs yawn'd, abysses blacken'd, caverns deep
Open'd into the hollow of the crags,
And down the abysses cataracts leapt with hair
Foam-white that flash'd behind them, and there came
A sound and motion as of wings of birds
Beating the darkness; so that unaware
My head swam, and methought I should have fallen

Into the precipices under us,
But even as I totter'd Nightshade's hand
Grasp'd and upheld me.
                    'Courage!' he exclaim'd,
'And fear not; what thou dreadest is the abyss
Of thought within thee! Follow fearlessly,
And look not downward!'
                    Crag was piled on crag
Above us, precipice on precipice
Swam dizzily beneath us; but as one
Who clings to a magician's robe, I gript
My Guide, and walk'd in safety till we gain'd
A place of caverns where like living ghosts
Wild shadows came and went; and in the void
Above those caverns lay an open space
Night-black and scrawl'd with starry zodiac signs;
And faint lights of the far-off universe
Came, went, and came again, and in the void
The tremulous pulses of the eternal Light
Were visibly throbbing!
                    Shuddering and afraid,
I cried, 'What realm is this? and who are these
That are as living things and come and go?'
And Nightshade answer'd: ''Tis the peaceful realm
Where with her crying children darkly dwells
The midnight mother, Meditation;

And what thou now dost see, or seem to see,
Is the dim conflict of unconscious shapes
In act to be!' And as he spake he pass'd
Into the shadow of a cave wherein
There sat a creature shapen like a man
But wan as any moonbeam; and methought
Its face was misted with a vaporous veil
Through which its eyes shone dimly, while its lips
Moved to wild music, and 'twas thus it sang:—

>   I am lifted on the wind
>   Of a thought as fleet as fire,
>   No foothold can I find,
>   But the wings of my desire
>   Beat the troubled air and gleam
>   With the dripping dews of dream!
>
>   I can hear the deep low thunder
>   Of the strong wheels of the sun,
>   I can see the green earth under,
>   As a golden ball is spun,
>   Rolling softly round and round
>   To a sweet and showery sound.
>
>   Life and Death unto my seeing
>   Are as vapours roll'd afar,
>   Through their folds the sea of Being,
>   With God's secret like a star
>   Shining o'er it, dark doth beat
>   'Neath the winds below my feet.

I am trancèd into fear
   Of mine own swift-striking wings,
For I hover darkly here,
   And the mystic cloud of things
Swims around me, and my brain
Trembles drenchèd with their rain.

And I cannot pause to think,
   But my wings must beat and beat;
If I pause for breath I sink
   To the Ocean at my feet—
With the wings of my desire,
On a wind as swift as fire,

I must struggle; and my thought
   Gathers naught from my soul's sight—
Only shadows star-enwrought,
   Death and Birth and Dawn and Night,
And the soft ecstatic motion
Of the Star above the Ocean.

Could I pause a little space,
   Could I pause a space and listening,
With that starlight on my face,
   See it glistening and glistening,
I could comprehend full plain
All the spirit seeks in vain.

But the wind whereon I sail
   Is as terrible as fire,
And I walk the winds, but fail
   With the wings of my desire,

And I swoon and seem to sink
On the mighty Ocean's brink.
And the cold breath of that Ocean
   Lingers wildly in my hair,
And that strange Star's rhythmic motion
   Soothes my passionate despair,
And on that one Star I call,
As I fall and fall and fall!

The wild strain ceasing, from the caves and crags
There came the cries of other piteous voices
Blent in one murmur like the clangour cold
Of numerous ocean waves; and as I paused
In terror, watching those phantasmic shapes,
One like a naked man pass'd by me shrieking
And plunged to some black gulf that yawn'd beneath;
And standing on the verge of the abyss
Another, like the spirit of the torrent,
Paused gazing upward with great sightless eyes,
And pointed at the lights of heaven, and moan'd:—

   The Woof that I weave not
     Thou wearest and weavest,
   The Thought I conceive not
     Thou darkly conceivest;
   The wind and the rain,
     The night and the morrow,
   The rapture of pain
     Fading slowly to sorrow,

> The dream and the deed,
>   The calm and the storm,
> The flower and the seed,
>   Are thy Thought and thy Form.
> I die, yet depart not,
>   I am bound, yet soar free,
> Thou art and thou art not,
>   And ever shalt be!

Ev'n as he spake there flash'd across the peaks
A Spectre such as timid cragsmen see
Flashing upon the Brocken overhead:
So near, it lit the chasms and the peaks,
So far, it seem'd a comet far away!
Clear yet transparent, pale though phosphorescent,
It stream'd across the darkness terribly,
Fading and changing; now a formless thing,
Trembling and meteoric, then, a space,
Bright as a wingèd beast of burning gold;
Then kindling into human lineaments,
Wild locks, outstretching hands; and then again
Melting to fiery vapour and departing
Swift as a shooting star; and as it changed
Those spirits from their caves peer'd out and wail'd,
And splendour as of sunrise lit the crags
And show'd the continents and seas beneath,
The silver'd map of the dark sleeping world;

And thunders from the heavens and earth beneath
Clash'd loud together, and the face of night
Was hidden, and from out the depths of life
There came the moans of countless weary men.

'Behold,' cried Nightshade, lit from head to feet
By that strange miracle of light, 'Behold
The Spectre of the Inconceivable!
The Light that flaming on the shuddering sense
Within us fades, but flash'd from soul to soul
Illumes that infinite ocean of sad thought
We sail and sail for ever and find no shore!
The Dream, the Dream! The Light that is the Life
Within us and without us, yet eludes
Our guessing—fades and changes, and is gone!'

Ev'n as he spake the light illumining
His form grew dimmer, and his face shone pale,
The shadows deepen'd, and the stars again
Lifted their silvern lids to gaze upon us,
While like a meteor that strange Portent fled
And darkness dwelt upon the lonely peaks.

BOOK XIII.

THE OPEN WAY.

WHEN I awaken'd, wakening still in dream,
   Methought that I was frail and bent with
      years,
And on a road that wound through a green vale
Slowly I trod, with pilgrim's staff and scrip,
While far away o'er dimly lightening hills
The rosy hand of Dawn closed softly o'er
One fluttering moth-like star; and as the light
Grew clearer, on a bank I sat me down
To watch the coming day, and rest and muse.
'Another day' (ev'n thus my musings ran)
'Another coming of a dewy day
After a night of pain! Once more above
The radiant rose of heaven openeth,
Petal by petal, glimmering in the dew;
Once more the lark arises paramount;
Once more the clouds move like a flock of sheep
Shepherded by the gentle summer wind.

The darkness is behind me, and I wake.
The way winds fresh before me, and I live.
O God! O Father! if indeed Thou art,
O Face beyond the Phantom! much I fear
My feet fail, while Thy City yet is far!
The world is green as ever, and the way
Sweeter by reason of those perils past ;
Yet on my hair the snow falls, in mine eyes
Thy dust is blown. Now I perceive full well
I set my soul upon a life-long quest
Which faileth if I pause before the end,
And yet my strength fails and my feet are sore
And surely I grow gray before my time.
Now of my weary journey nought remains
But babble of voices, glimmering of ghosts,
Tumult of shadows, with an under-sense
Of fair progressions moving to dim ends
Across a sad and problem-haunted world.
Much certes have I learn'd to make me wise,
Little to make me glad ; yet now I see
The green earth dripping balmy from the bath
Of orient, smiling ; but my soul for smiles
Is now too weary. Once my soul rejoiced
To drink the breath of each new dawn, to feel
The passion and the radiant power of life,
But now 'tis otherwise. The mask of Nature

Is beautiful—yea, far more beautiful
Than aught that I have known in happy dreams,
Yet seeing that I know it for a mask,
I love it less; and through its sockets shine
The Eyes behind, with portent horrible
And dangerous expectation. Help me, Lord!
For I am sick and weary of the way.'

O bright the morning came, as brightly shining
Upon the trembling murtherer's raiséd hair
As on the little clench'd hand of the babe
Smiling in sleep! softly the white clouds sail'd,
Edged with vermilion, to the east; the mists
Rose like white altar-smoke from that green vale,
The forests stirr'd with numerous leafy gleams,
The birch unbound her shining hair, the oak
Shone in his tawny mail, and from the wood
The brook sprang laughing; and above the fields
The lark rose, singing that same song it sang
On Adam's nuptial morn! Fresh, fair, and green,
Glisten'd that valley—only here and there
A little fold of morning vapour clung
To curtain yet some dewy mystery;
But through these folds of mist peep'd shining
    spires,
Fir tops as green as emerald, rookeries

Loud with the cawing rooks. In the damp fields
The mottled cattle gleam'd, while o'er the style
The shepherd, yawning with a fresh red face,
Came ankle-deep in dew.
                              Then I beheld
The vale was populous, for here and there
In straight lines upward through the dead still air
The smoke of quaint and red-tiled hamlets rose,
And mossy bridges arch'd like maidens' feet
Spann'd still canals whereon, by stout steeds drawn,
Moved broad boats piled with yellow scented hay.
And soon my heart took cheer, and as I went,
Half sad, half merry, to myself I sang
This ditty of the sunshine and the dawn :—

> Pleasant blows the growing grain,
> Golden, scented with the rain ;
>   Pleasant soundeth the lark's song
>   O'er the open way.
>
> Pleasant are the passing folk,
> Russet gown and crimson cloak,
>   To and fro they pass along
>   All the summer day.
>
> I can hear the church bells sound
> From the happy thorpes around ;
>   Men and maidens, old and young,
>   Flock afield full gay.

> Sweet is sunshine on the lea,
> Sweet it is to hear and see,
> Sweet it were to join the throng,
> If my soul could stay!

So sang I, hastening by the open road,
And all my heart was quicken'd twentyfold
Because of brightness and a pleasant place;
But even as I sang I overtook
A wight who walking slowly seem'd to brood
In potent meditation, downcast-eyed.
And with no sign I would have pass'd him by,
Scarce noting the calm brow and clear-cut cheeks,
Had not the stranger raised his eyes and smiled
Calm greeting such as fellow-scholars gave,
Half absently, when pacing slow within
The groves of Academe; whereat, indeed,
My feet began to pause unconsciously,
And my looks question'd of the pale cold face;
The dreamless eyes, the calm unruffled brow,—
For all was restless trouble in my soul,
Yet these seem'd peaceful as a woodland well.

Now, seeing my perplexity, once more
The stranger smiled, saying: 'Good morrow, Sir,—
A scholar, I presume? and by thy guise
A dweller in some city by the sea?

But wherefore in such haste?'
                    Then I replied:
'Because the hunger and the thirst divine
Consume me, and with sleepless feet I seek
The City of the Lord.'

STRANGER.

                    Nay, pardon me—
What City, friend? and furthermore, what Lord?

THE PILGRIM.

The Lord of Light, whose name is Beautiful.
Thou smilest. Is thy soul so desolate
That it hath never heard the name of God?

STRANGER.

Not so. I know the names of God full well.
But which god? There are many, I believe.

THE PILGRIM.

There is one God which made the heavens and earth,
The air, the water, all that in them is.

STRANGER.

In sooth? Hast thou beheld Him with thine eyes?

The Pilgrim.
Nay; none may look upon His face and live.

Stranger.
Thou hast not seen Him yet thou sayest He is,
He whom thou hast not seen?

The Pilgrim.
      I say again,
No mortal may behold Him and endure.

Stranger.
If thou hast not beheld Him for thyself,
How knowest thou that? Upon what testimony?

The Pilgrim.
Upon the testimony of His works—
Yonder wide heaven, this green-hollow'd earth;
His footprints on the rocks and on the sands;
His finger-touch o' nights when I sleep sound
(Yet start on being touch'd and waken up
With empty arms!); His seal on dead men's
  graves;
His signs, His portents, His solemnities.

STRANGER.

'Tis strange; for I have search'd as close as thou,
Deeper than most, aided by such wise lore
As lieth in the circles of the schools—
I have found naught, where thou hast found so much.

THE PILGRIM.

Dost thou deny Him?

STRANGER.

Nay, by Epicurus!
Logician am I and philosopher:
What, on the one side, cannot be affirm'd,
Can never be denied, upon the other.

THE PILGRIM.

I will accost thee in a rounder way.—
Canst thou keep calm, canst thou sleep sound o'
    nights,
Indifferent whether there be God or no?

STRANGER.

And I will answer thee as roundly, friend.
But first, permit me to disclose my name,
My calling, and the business I pursue.

The Open Way.

I am a scholar, christen'd Lateral,
Truth-speaker, dweller on the open way.
Much have I read in books, and more in men,
Far have I wander'd, deeply have I weigh'd
The words and ways of pilgrims passing by;
And much, I grant thee, they have blown abroad
This rumour of a City and a God:
Sometimes a City and a God; ofttimes
A God without a City; but a God
Invariably. Nay, in earlier days
I was beguiled out of the open way
To seek Him: in full daylight, diligently,
I sought Him, and I swear I found Him not;
Nor did I seek Him blindly, nor by night,
But in full daylight, on the public road.
I do not say, He is not; this I say:
To *me* He is not, being thus unseen.
And thou hast said, None may behold this God,
Because the sight would wither up the eyes;
But as I am a scholar, I affirm
There is no sight of all that I have seen
So dazzling that mine orbs endured it not.
What can be seen is harmless to the eyes,
Since what the eyes can see the eyes can bear.'

Thereon I mused (methought) with darken'd brow,

Then said: 'Dost thou know one Iconoclast?
Meseems that thou hast learn'd his lessons well.'

But Lateral cried, with wave of his white hand,
'I know the man thou meanest—know of him
Much good, some ill—but they would stone him here,
Where I walk free, upon the open way.
He gibes at all things, I at no thing gibe,
But measure all men's problems logically,
Not mocking, but in truthful reverence.'

We twain, thus talking, wander'd side by side,
And groups of men and women pass'd us by
In silence, as on harvest labour bent,
And many greeted Lateral by name.
Then as the toilworn congregation grew,
I ask'd, 'What folk are these who come and go?'
And Lateral in a low voice replied:
'Friend, some of these are Pilgrims like thyself
Whom I most courteously have spoken with,
Persuading them, whatever they believe,

That labour near the open way is best;
And lo! they leave the riddle of the gods
And quench their sad desires in blessèd toil.'

Whereon I cried: 'Hast thou search'd every-
   where?'
And 'Yea,' said Lateral; when solemnly,
With mine uplifted finger pointing back,
I cried: 'Raise now thine eyes to yonder peaks
Of mountain crested with eternal snow—
Hast thou sought *there?*' And Lateral answer'd:
   'Nay!
I am a dalesman, no mad mountaineer,
Nor do I deem a God, if God there be,
Would hang His glory like an icicle
Out of the common sunlight!'
                              ' Raise thine eyes,'
I answer'd, in a whisper thick with awe;
' Hast never, in the darkness, seen His feet
Flash yonder, like the flashing of a star?
Or 'midst the hush of a still frosty night
Hast thou not seen Him from afar, swathed
   round
With moonlight, lying like a corpse asleep
Upon the silence of the untrodden peaks,
With lights innumerable round His head

Blowing blue i' the wind? or hast thou never
    mark'd
A motion, the white waving of a Hand?'

Then Lateral, discerning in mine eyes
Who spake the tumult of a maniac pain,
Gently replied: 'I should have told thee, friend,
I am close-vision'd: what I see full nigh,
I see full clear, but these poor eyes of mine
Have never reach'd to the cold realm of ghosts.'

Then did I laugh in scorn. 'Blind human mole,
Dull burrower in the darkness! not for thee
God's glimmer, or the secret of the stars.
I see in thee the sexton of the creeds—
A cold and humourous knave, with never a guess
Beyond his spade and the cold skull it strikes
In digging his own grave. But fare thee well—
Our paths part here.'
                    I spake, and on I ran,
Leaving the pallid scholar far behind.

And as I pass'd along the open way,
I met on every side the drowsy stare
Of bovine human faces, heard the hum
Of hollow human voices; here and there

From bushy thickets peep'd a peaceful spire,
And oftentimes a church-bell rang, and folk
Came thronging unto prayer.
                      Then, slackening pace,
Darkling I mused. 'They toil, and pray together
In intervals of toil; and yet meseems
Their toil and prayer are cold mechanic things,
Since on no face there lieth any light
Of expectation, hope, or bright resolve.
Happy they seem; and happy are the beasts
They yoke for labour in the water'd meads;
And with the reverent habit of the sense
They soothe the solemn motions of the soul.'
And, looking round, on every side I sought
Some pilgrim with a heaven-seeking face,
But found none: only harvest-hoping eyes,
And lips compress'd with thoughts of golden gain.

At last, grown weary of the open way,
I turn'd aside, prest through a quickset hedge,
And over meads that rose to sunny slopes
Began with careless idle feet to fare;
But resting on my staff from time to time,
Drawing deep breath, I watch'd the winding road
Crowded with men and women of the vale.
Sweet were the slopes I trod with grass and thyme,

And cool the clear air blew from bank to bank
Of crowsfoot flowers; and as I went I cried:
'O gladder this than is the open way,
The common level road of tilth and toil—
For men are foolish, weak, and miserable,
Gazing straight downward like to blindest beasts,
Yoked to the ploughshare and prick'd forward ever
By base ignoble goads!'
                        Even as I spake,
I saw, upon a green bank in the sun
Beside a running brook, a curious wight
Who lying on his belly half asleep
Heard the brook gurgle in a gentle dream,
Yet read or seem'd to read an open Book
Set among scatter'd lilies on the grass.
He, looking upward as I slowly came,
Smiled like an infant or a heathen god
Calm and complacent in its gilded niche,
And nodded greeting supercilious
With half-shut eyes; and him I gazed upon
Awhile in silence, breathing from the ascent,
Then question'd:—
                  'Who art thou that lyest here
Close to the tumult of the open way,
Lord of thyself and pitiful to scorn
Of those who all around thee like to bees

Throng in and out the hive? What man art thou,
And what is that great Book which thou dost
    read?'

Then smiling softly, with the studied scorn
Of perfect courtesy, the man replied:
'I am a student, Microcos by name,
Who, scorning babble and the popular voice,
Dwell in the certainty of summer meads
Scarce vex'd by fear of thunder; and in this
    Book—
Observe it—old it is and worm-eaten—
Writ in the common tongue and therewithal
Dear to the common folk, I smiling read
Strange, sweet, old tales of God.' Thereon I said,
Stretching mine arms out with a weary cry:
'Thou art the man I seek, for surely thou
Must know the magic that makes conscience clear,
And as with nard and frankincense anoints
The sad worn feet of Woe. Unfold to me
Thy knowledge and the knowledge of thy Book.'

But Microcos uplifted a white hand
In protestation. 'Friend,' he said, 'be calm.
Dark on thy tired eyes lies dust of earth,
And on thy tongue the echoes of the road

Ring hollow yet. Mark me, the sweet blue sky
Was ne'er yet mirror'd in a broken water!
And for the blesséd knowledge thou dost seek
Calm is the consecration! Sit awhile
Beside me on the greensward by the brook,
And mark the white clouds sailing overhead,
The blue sky misted with its own soft breathing,
Then while the brook sings and from yonder comes
Subdued by distance the deep hum of men,
Let us together read a little space
The Legend of the Book.'
      Methought I stretch'd
My weary limbs upon the velvet sward,
And watch'd the white clouds sailing overhead,
The blue sky misted with its own soft breathing;
Then listen'd to the murmur of the brook,
And heard the cries of mortals faint as dream,
While in a low voice Microcos intoned,
With white forefinger on the stainéd page.
But scarcely had he turn'd one fluttering leaf,
When with a moan of wonder and of pain
I leapt up, wildly crying: 'Peace! O peace!
'Tis the same Legend I so oft have read—
The same dark Legend that hath made men mad—
No more, no more!'

MICROCOS.

        Now verily I perceive
The ways of unbelief have darken'd thee.
Sweet is the Book, read sweetly, in sweet
    weather.
O listen, and thy soul will be at peace.

THE PILGRIM.

Peace! Who names peace? O man! the words
    thou readest
Are as a whirlwind on a battle plain,
And every letter on that printed page
Is red as blood. How canst thou sit and smile,
And 'mid that carnage of the stainéd leaves
Sit as a dove that o'er its own voice broods
Perch'd on the red mouth of a murther'd man?

MICROCOS.

Meseems the Book is very beautiful,
Read in the light of Beauty, beautifully.
It tells of God, who framed the heavens and
    earth,
Who made Himself a sorrow and a sword,
Who lash'd Euroclydon unto his grip,
And 'mid the fiery smoke of sacrifice

Sat as the Sphynx with cold eternal eyes
Outlooking on his pallid worshippers.
Nay, further, of that same strange God it tells
Who clothed Himself with our humanity
As with a garment, drank the running brook,
And pass'd, a wan Shape waving feeble hands,
Silently thro' the very gates of Death!

The Pilgrim.

That God I seek! O if these things be true,
Instruct me—let me look upon His face!
Thou smilest. Read the riddle of thy smile.

Microcos.

I smile because thou comest fresh from paths
Where Literal and Lateral (the drones!)
Interpret the dry letter of the Book.
I tell thee, friend (now hear and be at peace!),
These things are phantasies and images
As unsubstantial as the dream I dream
Stretch'd here beside the babbling of the brook;
Yet sweeter, being dream: yea, no less sweet
Than moonlight, or the wonder of the flower,
Or aught of beautiful or terrible
That haunts the regions of the earth or air.

The Pilgrim.

Where is this God? I care not by what name
Ye know Him—Beautiful or Terrible?
Where is this God? and is He God at all?

Microcos.

I have not seen Him, and I know Him not.

The Pilgrim.

Dost thou believe He is? or dost thou read
A fable, disbelieving that He is?
For either all that Book is dust and lies,
Or else there was a Father and a Son—
A cruel Father and an outcast Son
The story of whose tears on this sad earth
Is there in words of wonder written down.

But with a dreamy smile the wight replied:
'These things I understand not; this I know—
Sweet is the Book, read sweetly, in sweet weather.
I prithee quit my sunshine!' Thereupon
He turn'd his back, and on his elbows leaning,
Smiled and read on,—while with a bitter cry
I left him, and ascended the green hill
Close to whose feet he lay.

       Meseem'd I climb'd
Through verdurous ways for hours until I reach'd
The grassy summit; there methought I found
A man in ragged raiment all alone;
And lo, his face was set as is a star
In contemplation of some far-off thing
Down in a valley underneath his feet.
Nor when I near'd him did he turn or speak,
But sadly gazed; and following his gaze
Mine eyes saw nothing but afar away
What seem'd a shining cloud.
        I touch'd his arm
And question'd: ' What is that thou gazest on?'

And he replied, not looking in my face:
' The City without God, where I was born.'

BOOK XIV.

THE CITY WITHOUT GOD.

BEAUTEOUS and young, yet bent as with the load
Of weary years, pale as a wintry May
When lingering frosts silver the path that leads
To brightness of the flowering summer meads,
Was he who spake: his locks of tender gold
Sadden'd with gleams of grey, his great blue eyes
Pallid and dim with melancholy light,
His voice forlorn yet sweet; and by a chain
He held a snow-white lamb that stood beside him
And gently lick'd his thin transparent hand.

I echoed him: 'The City without God!
Alas! what City?' 'Yonder,' he replied,
'Behold it gladdening in the light of day!'

So saying, he pointed downward, and behold!
I saw the gleam of shining roofs and walls
Below me on the plain; and fair they seem'd

As any upbuilt by hands, and thitherward
Ran divers ways with thronging crowds that
    seem'd,
Seen from that hilltop, small as creeping ants.
He stood as moveless as a marble man
Down gazing, while I question'd: 'Weary years
I have sought the City of God and found it not.
Who built this other underneath God's heaven?'

He answer'd, keeping still his misted eyes
Fix'd on the vision: 'They who built the City
First laid the shadowy ghosts of all the gods,
And, lastly, God the Father's; then they
    wrought
Beneath the empty void and drain'd the marsh,
And out of earth quarried the marble bones
Of buried æons, and with blood and tears
Cemented them together, and at last,
Strange as a dream, the City of Man uprose.'

THE PILGRIM.

How fair it seems! yea, even fairer far
Than the proud City of Christopolis!
And thither hasten crowds as eagerly
As happy people making holiday!

THE STRANGER.

From every corner of the earth they throng,
Hearing the joyful music of the bells
Proclaiming that the reign of God is done!
I woke to that same music long ago,
Nor wonder'd, tho' mine ears had never heard
The name of any God, nor knew of any,
Save the great Spirit of Man; and when I ran
A child along the golden streets, and saw
The air alive with shining argosies,
The ways all beautiful, the temples fill'd
With sunshine and with music, I rejoiced
As only children may; but presently,
Ere yet I grew to the full height of man,
There came a wight in pilgrim's weeds like thine
Who told me of strange Cities far away
Where God still reign'd, and of the woeful Valley
Still haunted by the shadows of dead gods,
And suddenly, out of a gate in heaven,
A piteous Face Divine look'd down upon me
And vanish'd; and from that dark hour I knew
No gladness in the shining of the sun.

His voice was as a cry upon a mountain
Far off and faint, yet clear; and as he ended

He turn'd his eyes upon me, dim with tears,
Then said: 'Retrace thy steps and hasten back!
Better the woefulest cities thou hast seen
Than yonder happy City of Despair!'
Whereat I cried: 'Since in Christopolis
No comfort dwells, but only (as I have seen)
A blood-red crucifix upon a grave,
And since my weary flight has ranged the world,
Seeking in vain a City upbuilt by God,
I will go down to yonder City of Man
And therewithin find some calm place of rest;
For they who built it up so bright and fair
Must of all men be closest kin to gods
In love, in wisdom, and in mastery.'

He answer'd: 'Search the City if thou wilt,
And I will guide thee thither; yet be warn'd,—
No Pilgrim God hath haunted out of hope
Ever abides among those shining walls;
For if they slay him not, or if he 'scapes
Their melancholy prisons of the mad,
He flies into the wastes beyond the City
And nevermore returns.'
                        Then side by side
We pass'd descending towards the open way
Crowded with wayfarers; and as we went

The splendour of the City dazzled me
Like the great golden lilies of the dawn;
And presently we reach'd the living river
Which swept us onward till I saw full clear
The marvel of the domes that man had built.

Even as I paused in wonder, crying aloud
' Rejoice! for, lo, I have found at last a City
More beauteous far than any built by gods!'
I turn'd to share my joy with that pale wight
Who had led me thither, but his face and form
Had vanish'd in the crowd surrounding me,
And into those bright streets I pass'd alone.

Thus wandering on I joyfully discern'd
The white and shining walls, the flashing roofs,
Of that great City; not so fair, meseem'd,
As far-off splendours of Christopolis,
Yet stately, calm, and beautiful indeed,
With marble palaces in stately squares,
Broad streets with glad green trees on either side,
Bright gardens, leaping fountains, temples, fanes,
Observatories lifted high in air
Near to the sun and stars,—all beauty and grace
Of earthly cities builded up by hands;
No walls it had, nor gates of brass or stone,

But mighty avenues on either side
Where all might enter in; and as I went
I pass'd the citizens in snowy robes
Going and coming calmly in the sun.

Brighter, and ever brighter, as I went
Grew the full sunlight of the shining place;
And as I wander'd through the bright broad streets
With leafy colonnades on either side,
And saw the stately white-robed citizens,
Peaceful and gentle, moving to and fro,
And watch'd o'erhead the many-colour'd ships
Wingéd like eagles sailing hither and thither,
My sorrow lessen'd and my fears grew cold.
For surely never City of the earth
Was brighter and more fair!—Down every street
A cooling rivulet ran, and in the squares
Bright fountains sparkled; and where'er I walk'd
The library, the gymnasium, and the bath
Were open to the sun; virgins and youths
Swung in the golden air like wingéd things,
Or in the crystal waters plunged and swam,
Or raced with oiléd limbs from goal to goal;
And in the hush'd and shadowy libraries,
Or in the galleries of painted art,
Or in the dusk museum, neophytes

Walk'd undisturb'd; and never sound of war,
Clarion or trumpet, cry of Priest or King,
Came to disturb the City's summer peace;
And never a sick face made the sunlight sad,
And never a blind face hunger'd for the light,
And never a form that was not strong and fair
Walk'd in the brightness of those golden streets.

Then thought I, 'Fairer at least and happier
This City is than was Christopolis,
For all that dwell herein are strong and free!'
And as I spake I saw afar away
The reddening sunset and the approaching night;
When, suddenly, ere the dark night could fall,
Radiance like sunlight from a thousand lamps
Flooded the bosom of the wondrous City
And made it bright as dawn!
                              Methought I sat
Out in the brightness of a mighty square,
And watch'd the light and airy argosies
Quietly sailing 'gainst the shadow'd sky,
Now rising, now descending, even as birds,
With some fresh freight of men beneath their wings;
But as I mused I heard a sudden roar
As of a tide of life fast flowing thither,
And soon a crowd of white-robed citizens

Surged wildly round me, bearing in their midst
That pallid wight whom I had mark'd at morn
Leading his flower-deck'd lamb; and many hands
Were reach'd unto him, to grasp or strike him down,
And crying wildly to my side he ran
And saying, 'Help me, brother!' fell and knelt,
Grasping my robe.
     Then, as the crowd swept down,
I faced them, saying, 'Stand back, and touch him not!
Children of freedom, citizens of peace,
Why are your spirits vex'd against this man?'
Then one, a reverent wight with beard like snow,
Stepp'd from their ranks and answer'd: .' Give him
  to us!
He hath profaned our temples, and is mad.'

THE PILGRIM.

What would ye with him? Back, and answer me!

CITIZEN.

Strange to this City must thou be indeed,
Not knowing that its rulers, holy men,
Endure not in the shrines or public ways
The hideousness of disease or pestilence,
Nor any sight of moral leprosy,

Nor any form of spiritual taint
Whereof men surely die. Give up the man;
We shall not slay him, but deliver him
To those who in our public hospitals
Are the approved physicians of the soul.

The Pilgrim.

Name me his madness ere I yield him up,
And give me proof of his profanity.

Citizen.

The proof is simple. Through our streets he walk'd
Crying on some wild spectre of the brain,
Yea, naming an old name of little meaning,
The name of God, which (as our granddames tell)
Was in the olden times of ignorance
By nurses used to quiet children with;
Moreover, having enter'd unperceived
One of our holy Hospitals of Birth
Wherein the wheat is winnow'd from the tare,
The strong life from the weak, he straightway
    raved
And in the name of that same God blasphemed!

Then stooping down to him who clutch'd my robe,

I question'd saying, 'Brother, are these things
    true?'
And like a man whose face is blanchéd still
From some strange sight of horror infinite,
He wail'd reply:—

                    'Ah, God! it haunts me still!
The darken'd hall, the devils stoled in black,
The cries of little children newly born,
And from the distant darkness the low moans
Of woeful mothers! Brother, stoop thy head
And listen!—As they bare the sweet babes in,
Methought they look'd like angels newly fallen,
Tender as rose-leaves, from the hands of God;
And some were strong, and drew great draughts of
    life,
And these they spared; but some were weak and
    frail,
Poor little waifs with sad dim heavenly eyes,
And these, being tried with delicate instruments,
Were straightway still'd, and quickly swept away
Like useless leaves, for instant burial;
And some were blind, and since they could not see,
They threw them into darkness with the rest!
Then, brother, looking on that piteous sight,
Seeing the little children cast away,
I hid my face, and call'd aloud on God!

CITIZEN.

You hear him. Yea, he raves! And such as he,
In name of that effete and loathsome Christ
Who made of this sweet world a lazar-house,
Would swarm our streets with sick and halt and lame,
And give our precious birthright to the blind!

THE PILGRIM.

Take heed, lest thou thyself blaspheme and rave!

CITIZEN.

How now? Dost thou defend and justify him?

THE PILGRIM.

Would 'twere as easy a task to justify
Meters and measurers of the flesh and soul;
For if these things he saith be true indeed
'Tis your archpriests who are surely mad, not he;
For who, beholding any thing new-born,
Be it fair or frail, happy or miserable,
Shall say what soul may grow from such a seed?
And who shall know but the infirmest flesh,
Though dark and dumb as any chrysalis,
May hold the strongest and the surest wings
That ever rose to the clear air of heaven?

Nay, who shall tell what light *we* cannot see
Whose orbs see only earth and earthly things
Steals through the darken'd casements of those eyes
Whereon the Hand divine hath drawn a veil?

Citizen.

Beware to echo him and share his blame!

The Pilgrim.

He cried to God, and God shall hear his cry!
I join my voice to his, and cry a curse
On this your City, fouler far to God
(If these sad things he saith be true indeed)
Than Sodom, which He did destroy by fire!

Citizen.

Another madman! Brethren, grasp them both!

The Pilgrim.

Yea, seize us and destroy us, since ye slay
The little crying helpless seed of Him
Who in His pity made Himself a Child!
O God, Who made the lambkin and the babe,
And fill'd the great heart of the martyr'd babe
With human dews of love and gentleness,

So that He grew the help and friend of man—
O God, whose smile was for the sick and sad,
The halt, the lame, the wretched, and the blind,
Put out Thy hand to help Thy little ones,
And gnaw to death with Thine avenging worms
This Herod of the Cities in its pride!

Ev'n as I spake, with frantic prayers and cries,
Clasping that hunted brother in my arms,
They swept upon us and despite our shrieks
Tore us asunder, trampled under foot
The flower-fed lamb that gentle wanderer led,
And swept me cruelly I knew not whither.
Struggling amidst their throng, methought I swoon'd;
And when I open'd startled eyes once more
Methought that I was lying chain'd and bound
Within some lonely madhouse of the City!

How strange it seem'd that, ere my sense grew clear,
My eyesight ready to distinguish shapes,
I lay and listen'd to an old sweet hymn
Sung o'er my cradle when a little child!
And then I heard a sound like murmur'd prayer,
And louder singing as of angel-choirs.
Then, looking round, I saw that I was lying
Within a large and dimly-lighted hall,

And all around were human shapes like mine—
Women and men, some chain'd as I was chain'd,
And others moving ghostlike to and fro;
And from the throats of some of these there came
The murmur I had heard of hymn and prayer.
Gentle they seem'd, save one or two who shriek'd,
Gnash'd teeth, or tore their hair, crying aloud
Upon the God of Thunder. Some stood wrapt
Their eyes on some strange vision and their arms
Wildly outreaching; others knelt at prayer;
A few moved to and fro, with eyes cast down,
Musing and pale; and many told their beads.
Bare was the place—no picture hanging there,
Or any fair device to please the gaze;
But on the whitewash'd wall the mad folks' hands
Had written strange old names—of God the Lord,
Christ Jesus, Mary Mother, and the Saints;
And crouching in a corner one poor soul,
Dreaming aloud and muttering to himself,
Had drawn in charcoal Death the Skeleton,
Buddha as black as night but radiant-wing'd,
And Christ, with hanging head, upon His Cross.

Wondering and pitying I gazed around
Seeking some friendly face; and I beheld,
Standing close by me in a saffron robe,

A maiden like Madonna heavenly-eyed,
Her white hands folded meekly on her breast,
Praying and looking upward in a dream.
To her I spake, demanding reverently
What place it was wherein I prison'd lay,
And who my weary fellow-sufferers were
That in that dreary building flock'd together?

'Dear brother,' she replied, 'this is the place
Wherein those weary wights who are mad past cure
Are prison'd from the sunshine and sweet air;
All here are pilgrims like thyself, who seek
God and God's City, with assurance sweet
Of life immortal and eternal peace.'

The Pilgrim.

Then these are mad folk, and I, too, am mad?
And yet, meseems, though some are sad and wild,
Many are smiling, bright and well-content.

The Maiden.

Because each night, when all the doors are closed,
Fair angels fresh from heaven enter here;
Yea, even Christ the Lord doth often come
To comfort them in their extremity.

I gazed upon her wondering, and methought

Her azure eyes were strange and sweetly wild,
And patiently her bosom rose and fell
With some disturbing rapture of the soul;
Wherefore I cried:—
    'Alas! they are mad indeed!
Since they behold what is not, and perceive
That Phantom Christ whose other name is Death!'

THE MAIDEN.

Nay, they behold the eternal Light and Life,
Whose earthly name is Christ the Crucified!

THE PILGRIM.

Yet tell me, wherefore are they prison'd here?

THE MAIDEN.

Because the rulers of the City hold
That they are lepers, who, being suffer'd forth,
And speaking with the people in the streets,
Would spread their souls' disease a hundredfold.
If any man doth breathe the Name Divine,
Or seeing strange visions tell what he hath seen,
Or speak of lands of dream beyond the grave,
Straightway they lead him here, to these dark halls,
For inquisition.
   Even as she spake

The inquisitors appear'd, grave men and old
Array'd in solemn black, and usher'd in
By ceremonious guardians of the place;
But, save myself, methought, none heeded them,
All those pale prisoners being intent in prayer,
Or singing aloud, or trancéd into dream.
Then one, a keeper of the prison, led
The inquisitors to the corner where I lay,
And touching me upon the shoulder cried
'Stand up! and hearken!'—and still chain'd I
    rose
And faced them, while with calm and pitying eyes
They coldly read my face for testimony.
Then one said, smiling, 'Fear not! since we come
To heal thee, not to harm thee, if perchance
Thy grievous malady admits a cure.
Thou art one of those who darkening in a dream
See visions, and beyond these clouds of Time
Some phantom City builded upon air?'

Then I, forewarn'd and cunning to escape,
Smiled also: 'So they said who left me here;
And peradventure, when I first set forth
On the sad pilgrimage which brought me hither,
I saw such phantoms, dream'd such dreams, and
    raved;

But now, alas! the euphrasy of pain
Hath purged mine eyes of that ancestral rheum,
And what my soul once saw I see no more.'

'How now?' I heard them mutter among themselves,
'The man perchance is saner than we thought.'
And looking in my face, another said,
'Be sure, if thou art heal'd of thy disease
Thou shalt escape these chains and wander free.
Now answer!—What is highest of living things?'

THE PILGRIM.

Man; since he is the chief and lord of all.

INQUISITOR.

Whence comes he? whither goes he?

THE PILGRIM.

                                   Out of dust
He cometh, and full soon to dust returns.

INQUISITOR.

When Death hath broken the light vase of life,
What then remaineth?

The Pilgrim.

Ashes in an urn.

Inquisitor.

Think! When the body is dust, doth naught survive?

The Pilgrim.

Those thoughts which are the heirloom of us all,
The Spirit of Man which lives though men pass by.

Inquisitor.

Look round upon these souls which share thy prison—
What are they?

The Pilgrim.

Madmen.

Inquisitor.

Yea; but wherefore mad?

The Pilgrim.

Because they see a Shadow on the world,
Namely, the Shadow of Death, and call it God;
Because their prayers like fountains flash at heaven
And fall unanswer'd back upon the ground;

Because they, travelling in a desert place,
Behold the mirage of a City of Dream!

Then I perceived they look'd at one another,
Smiling well pleased, and presently they said :
' The man is surely harmless—let him go!'
And straightway I was free; but as I moved
In act to leave the place, the mad folk throng'd
Around me, crying the name of God aloud,
Rebuking and upbraiding; and one, the maid
With whom I first had spoken, moan'd in mine ear,
' God help thee! Since thou hast denied thy God,
Who now shall be thy succour and thy stay?'
As sick of soul and shamed I crept away,
I heard behind me from the madhouse walls
The murmur of a fountain of strong prayer,
Voices that sang, ' Hosannah to the Lord!
He hath built His City, and He calls us thither!'
And once again it seem'd the cradle-hymn
That I had heard when I was lying a babe
Fresh from the shores of some celestial sea ;
Wherefore my eyes grew dim with piteous tears,
And bowing down my head, I sobb'd aloud.

But bright as Hesper in the morning beams
The City sparkled—square and street and mart
Busy and merry, throng'd with white-robed crowds,

The blue air bright with happy argosies,
The water full of swimmers swift and nude,
The fountains leaping, and the hearts of all
Leaping in unison, while from countless choirs
A merry music rang! But all my soul
Was weary of gladness, and I long'd, methought,
To be alone with God; and seeing pass
One whose grave eyes seem'd sadder than the rest,
I touch'd him on the arm and said unto him,
'Prithee, are there no Temples in this City,
Wherein a soul worn out on pilgrimage
May rest a space and pray?' and he replied,
'Yea, truly—there are many—and yonder stands
One of our fairest'—pointing as he spake;
And I beheld a mighty edifice,
Its dome of azure enwrought with golden signs,
Stars, constellations, jewell'd galaxies,
And changeful symbols of the zodiac;
Over the columns of the portico
A frieze in marble—strong Asclepios
Pictured Apollo-like in godlike strength,
Dispensing herbs and healing crowds of sick,—
Τὸ ἀληθεύειν καὶ τὸ εὐεργετεῖν,
Written in golden letters underneath.

I climb'd the marble steps, and pushing back

The curtain on the threshold, enter'd in;
And in an instant, as one quits the sun
And steals 'mid umbrage where the light is strain'd
Thro' blood-red blooms and alabaster leaves,
I found myself alone in solemn shades.
Facing me to the eastward, whence the day
Crept thro' a stainéd window (figuring
The Sun himself burning with golden beams
And lighting globes of green and amethyst),
A solemn Altar, upon which there stood
The golden image of a sleeping Child,
And bending o'er the cradle where he lay
A Skeleton of silver, ruby-eyed;
And round the solemn place, to left and right,
Were many-colour'd windows limn'd whereon
Instead of saints were wise men of the earth—
Physicians azure-robed, astronomers
With stars for crowns, pale bards in singing robes,
And women like the sibyl, book in hand.
From some mysterious heart of this fair shrine
A solemn organ music slowly throbb'd,
With deep pulsations, like the sound o' the sea.
Then spirit-broken, awed and wondering,
I cast myself upon my face and pray'd;
And while I lay, methought, an unseen choir
Sang of primæval darkness suddenly

Struck by the golden ploughshare of the sun,
Of kindling azure fields where softly fell
The nebulous seeds that blossom'd into worlds,
Of dark transfigurations changing slowly
From rock to flower, from flower to things of life,
And through the mystic scale, from beasts to man;
And lo! meseem'd a darkness and despair,
O'ermastering, awe-compelling, creeping down
Like clouds that blacken from the mountain-peaks
And shroud the peaceful valleys, stole upon me,
And swathed my soul in dread before I knew,
So that I could not pray, nor knew indeed
What spirit to pray to or what god to praise,
For all I felt within and over me
Was some blind sense of demiurgic doom
Feeling with strange progressions up to life,
Then breaking, as a wave that breaks and goes!
Then cried I: 'Spirit of Man, if spirit thou art
That in this Temple broodest like a cloud,
Blind Spirit of Doom and Mystery and Change,
How shall I apprehend thee? Wrap thyself
In humble raiment of some awful god,
And I shall know thee; clothe thy ghost divine
In piteous limbs of white humanity,
Speak with a human whisper in mine ear,
And rest thy human hand upon my hair,

And I shall feel thy touch, and worship thee;
Come down, O God! if thou art quick not dead,
And walk as other gods have walk'd the world
With tread that thunders or with feet that bleed,
That I may feel thee pass and bow to thee—
For who shall worship darkness deep as death,
And silence still as stone, and dreariest dread,
Faceless and eyeless, formless, without bound?'
Thus praying, I was startled by a voice,
Angry though feeble, crying in mine ear,
'Arise! profane not with a foolish cry
This Temple of the Law!' and looking up,
I saw a woman very grey and old
Leaning upon a staff and gazing at me:
Her robe all black and wrought with starry signs
Like those upon the Temple's azure dome,
Her hair as white as wool, her wrinkled face
As blank and ashen-grey as is the Sphinx;
So strange and sinister her look, she seem'd
One of the fabled Mothers who for ever
Intone Cimmerean runes of death and birth.

'What woman art *thou?*' I cried, and she replied,
'A Virgin of the Temple; one whose task
'Tis to preserve the altar clean and pure,
And sweep the floor of dust. I heard thee praying

And came to warn thee hence; for prayers like thine
Offend the solemn Spirit of the place.'

THE PILGRIM.

Name me that Spirit, and I will pray to Him!

THE WOMAN.

Alack! no tongue hath named him, and no eye
Hath seen, no mortal known, the Unknowable;
But if thou needst must pray, give prayers to those
Who are pictured on the windows and the walls—
The blessèd men who by their thoughts and deeds
Have builded up this Temple of the Law.

THE PILGRIM.

Men that have perish'd! why should I pray to those,
Seeing I famish for the Imperishable?

THE WOMAN.

Aye me! the foolish hunger and the thirst
Of babes who sit before the laden board
And crave for fabled meat and drink of gods!
Take heed; for in a little while thine eyes
Shall close from seeing, and thy throat and ears
Be fill'd with dust. Death is the one thing sure,

And Death is here, the Shadow in the shrine!
Yet Death is but the shadow of a change,
Since naught that is departs, tho' all things die!

THE PILGRIM.

Thy words are dark as night. What meanest thou?

THE WOMAN.

Lives pass. The Spirit of Life alone survives.

THE PILGRIM.

Yea, and survives for ever, being God.

THE WOMAN.

There is no God, but only Death and Change.

THE PILGRIM.

Read me thy riddle, Mother Sibylline!

THE WOMAN.

The Darkness that for ever gathers here,
And in the heavens, and in the heart of man,
Is elemental; 'tis the primal force
For ever quickening into life and change,
For ever failing in a thousand forms,
And falling back to feed the central Heart

That throbs for ever thro' the flaming worlds.
Spark of that Heart, that heliocentric flame,
Art thou, who, being kindled for a moment,
Shalt vanish as a spark blown from a forge!

The Pilgrim.

Aye me!—only a spark, to flash and fade!

The Woman.

Nay, less!—this earth is but a flake of fire,
Fallen from the nearest of those flaming suns
Which burn a space and then like lesser lives
In their due season blacken and grow cold.
Think on thy littleness, thy feebleness,
And praise the mystic, all-pervading Law,
Which on the eyelids of unnumber'd worlds
Sheds the ephemeral life, the dust of Time.

The Pilgrim.

Alas! how should I praise the Invisible,
Which shows me baser than the dust indeed?
The empty Void shall never have my prayer,
But that which lifts me up and gives me wings,
And proves me more than any unconscious world
However luminous and beautiful,—
That will I worship. Fairer far, methinks,

The meanest, smallest, tutelary god
That ever gave men gifts of fruit and flowers,
The frailest spirit of human fantasy
Blessing the worshipper with kindly hands,
Than this dead Terror of the Inevitable,
Weighing like leaden Death, with Death's despair,
In the core of countless worlds! I ask for God,
For Light, not Darkness, and for Life, not Death;
Not for the fatal doom which leaves me low—
Nay, for the gentle, upward-urging Hand
Which lifts me on to immortality!

So saying, I left her standing sadly there,
And quitting that proud Temple fled again
Into the common sunlight; but my soul
Was sad as night and darken'd with a doubt,
And in my veins the ominous sense of doom
Was creeping like some cold and fatal drug;
So that the City with its thousand lights
Seem'd like a feeble taper flickering
In chilly winds of death, and all the throng
Moths hovering round a melancholy flame.
Faint was my spirit as a sickly light
Held in the night and shielded by thin hands
From the strong wintry wind, when presently
I mark'd another temple marble-wrought,

And seeing that the doors were open wide
Enter'd, and passed thro' echoing corridors,
And found myself within its inmost core.
And in a lofty hall, with marble paven,
One stood before a table wrought of stone
And strewn with phials, knives, and instruments
Of sharpest steel; before him, ranged in rows,
On benches forming a great semi-moon,
His audience throng'd, all hungry ears and eyes.
The man was stript to the elbow, both his hands
Were stain'd and bloody; and in the right he held
A scalpel dripping blood; beneath him lay,
Fasten'd upon the board, while from its heart
Flowed the last throbbing stream of gentle life,
A cony as white as snow. In cages near
Were other victims—cony and cat and ape,
Lambkins but newly yean'd, and fluttering doves
Which preen'd their wings and coo'd their summer cry.
The hall was darken'd from the sun, but lit
By lamps electric that around them shed
Insufferable brightness clear as day.

Presently at the door there enter'd one
Who by a chain did lead a gentle hound
Which scenting new-shed blood drew back in dread;
Whereon from all the benches rose a cry

Of cruel laughter; and the lecturer smiled,
And wiping then his blood-stain'd instrument
And casting down the cony scarcely dead,
Prepared the altar for fresh sacrifice.
The hound drew back and struggled with the chain
In act to fly, but roughly dragged and driven
He reach'd the lecturer's feet and there lay down,
Panting and looking up with pleading eyes;
The lecturer smiled again and patted him,
When lo! the victim lick'd the bloody hand,
Pleading for kindness and for pity still.
Then in my dream methought I heard a voice
Ring clearly and coldly as a churchyard bell,
Saying, 'Lo! our next subject, friends—a hound,
Chosen in preference even to the ape,
Because the convolutions of his brain
Are likest to the highest, even Man's!'

Suddenly in my vision I perceived
The victim's face, though hairy and hound-like still,
Was now mysteriously humanised
Into the likeness of a naked Faun,
Who pricking hairy ears and rolling eyes
Shriek'd with a sylvan cry! and at the sound
There came from all the cages round about
A murmur such as in the leafy woods

Comes rippling from the merry flocks of Pan;
Yea, I beheld them—cony and cat and ape,
And lo! the tamest and the feeblest there
Had ta'en the pretty pleading human looks
Of naiad babes and tiny freckled fauns,
Sweet elves and pigmy centaurs of the woods!
And when the victim moan'd, they answer'd him
With pitying babble of the unconscious groves,
Cries of the haunted forest, and such shrieks
As the pale dryad prison'd in the tree
Yields when the woodman stabs her milky bark;
And mingled with such piteous woodland sounds
There came a gentle bleating as of lambs,
Blent with another and a stranger sound,
Faint, as of infants crying for the breast!

This pass'd; for all my soul, being sick and sad,
Grew blinded with the fastly-flowing tears;
Yet straining once again my troubled sense
I saw the faun strapt down upon the board,
And though his feet were beast-like, his twain hands
Were human, and his fingers clutch'd the knife!
He shriek'd; I shriek'd in answer; and, behold,
His head turn'd softly, and his eyes sought mine.

Then, lo! a miracle—face, form, and limbs,

Changed on the instant—neither hound nor faun
Lay there awaiting the tormentor's knife,
But One, a living form as white as wax,
Stigmata on his feet and on his hands,
And on his face, still shining as a star,
The beauty of Eros and the pain of Christ!
I knew Him, but none other mortal knew,
Though every tiny faun and god o' the wood,
Still garrulously babbling, named the Name;
And looking up into the torturer's face
He wept and murmur'd, 'Even as ye use
The very meanest of my little ones,
So use ye Me!' That other smiled and paused—
He only heard the moaning of a hound—
Then crushing one hand on the murmuring mouth,
He with the other took the glittering knife,
And leisurely began!
      I look'd no more;
But covering up mine eyes I shriek'd aloud
And rush'd in horror from the accursèd place;
But at the door I turn'd, and turning met
The piteous eyeballs fix'd in agony
Beneath a forehead by the knife laid bare!
'Almighty God,' I cried, 'behold Thy Son!'
And pointed at the victim. As I spake,
A throng of frowning men surrounded me,

Crying, 'Who raves? down with him! drive him
    forth!'
And in an instant I was smitten and driven
Beyond the porch into the open air.
There stood I panting, dazzled by the day
Which burnt all golden in the paven square,
And gazing back upon the gloomy porch
As on the sulphur-spewing mouth of Hell.

Then one, a tall grave wight in priestly robes,
Strode to me, crying, 'Hence! profane no more
The Temple with thy presence!' but I call'd
My curse upon the place, and lifting hands,
Again cried out on God.

The Priest.

                What man art thou
That darest in this holy place blaspheme,
Knowing God is not, knowing the wise have
    proved
All gods to be a shadow and a snare?

The Pilgrim.

God is! He hears! O God, send down a sign
To slay these slaves who torture Christ Thy Son!

The Priest.

Wild is thy speech. What hast thou heard or seen,
To rob thee of thy wits and make thee mad?

The Pilgrim.

In there the Christ is worse than crucified;
He moans, He bleeds beneath the torturer's knife!

The Priest.

O fool! what is this Christ of whom you rave?
A man of Judah, who, being mad like thee,
Eighteen long centuries since was crucified,
And cried the self-same wild despairing cry
To God who could not, or who would not, hear?
What wrought he for the world? A net of lies!
What legacy bequeath'd he? Tears and dreams!
I tell thee, man, that those who uplight the knife
In this fair Temple of Humanity
Have heal'd more wounds in man's poor suffering
    flesh
Than e'er your Christ did open in man's soul.
Your God had sacrifice of lambs and beeves,
A holocaust whose smoke did blacken heaven!
We to a fairer god, the Spirit of Man,

Offer in love a few poor living things
Whose sufferings by use are sanctified.

The Pilgrim.

E'en as ye serve the meanest of his lambs,
So serve ye Christ, the Shepherd of the flock!

The Priest.

Man is the Shepherd of this world, and we
The friends and priests of Man; to Man alone
Belongs the privilege of dispensing pain;
All lower things are means and instruments;
And if to save him but a finger-ache
'Tis meet the baser types should bleed and die.
Look round upon this City! Years ago
Your Christ, a hideous Phantom, haunted it,
And in his train Disease and Pestilence,
Foulness and Fever, danced their dance of Death.
Our wise men came and drave the Phantom forth,
And since that hour the ways are bright and clean;
Disease is banish'd, Pestilence is now
An old man's memory, Death itself is turn'd
Into the servant and the slave of Man.

The Pilgrim.

Death comes indeed! Ye have not vanquish'd Death!

THE PRIEST.

Death is the holy usher stoled in black
Who cometh to the wearied out and old
Saying, 'Your bed is made—'tis time to rest!'
Right gladly to the solemn death-chamber
They follow, and are curtain'd in that sleep
Which never yet was stirr'd by man or God;
And yet they die not, since no force is lost,
But passeth on, and these survive for ever
In children ever coming, ever going,
To make the merry music of the world.

THE PILGRIM.

Merry, indeed!—made up of tears and moans,
Of fair things martyr'd, frail things sacrificed,
In name of that most cruel god of all,
The godless Spirit of Man! and lo! at last,
Your children are baptized with blood of beasts,
And heal'd with death of innocent childlike things,
And strengthen'd out of slaughter. Woe is me!
That ever child should draw his strength from death,
And be the heir of cruelty and pain!

Like one half waking and half sleeping, risen
From spirit-chilling visions of the night,

Uncertain of the world wherein he walks,
Haunted and clouded, thro' the City I pass'd;
And voices seem'd afar off, and all sounds
Ghostly and strange, and every face I met
Fantastic, melancholy, and unreal:
And weary hours pass'd by, and still I walk'd;
And in the end I found myself alone
Upon a green hillside beyond the town,
Entering a beauteous Garden of the Dead.

The place was green and still, with shadowy walks,
And banks of gracious flowers; and ranged in rows
Along the grassy terraces were placed
White urns that held the ashes of the dead,—
In each of these a handful white as salt
Left from the cleansing fire; and in the midst
There stood a building like a sepulchre
From the iron heart of which a pale blue flame
Rose strange and sacrificial; hither came
The bearers with their burdens linen-wrapt
Which being dropt into the furnace-flame
Shrivell'd like leaves and swiftly were consumed.
While near the fiery place I gazing stood
I saw from out the glistening gate of brass
An old man issue, naked to the waist,
And holding in his hands a silver urn.

Still darken'd and perplex'd I spake to him,
And when he answer'd, setting down the urn
And gazing at me with lacklustre eyes,
His voice seem'd ghostly, faint, and far away.
'Art thou the sexton of this place?' I cried;
And straightway he replied, wiping his brows,
'Adam the Last, the watcher of the fire—
That is my name and office, gentle sir.'

THE PILGRIM.

So, Adam, last or first, the old order stands?
Your masters have not yet abolish'd Death!

ADAM.

Nay, God forbid! (alas! the foolish name
I learnt when I was young!)— Death comes to all;
The one thing sure and best—man's Comforter!

THE PILGRIM.

Can men that are so merry, having upbuilt
A City so serene and beautiful,
Still welcome silence and the end of all?

ADAM.

Yea, verily—though should they hear me breathe
The dreary truth, the rulers of the City

Might rob me of mine office, gentle sir;
But by thy face and raiment I perceive
Thou art a stranger, coming from the land
Of gracious gods and old, where I was born.
Fair is the City, as thou sayest, and merry,
Yet many men grow weary of its mirth,
And ere their time would gladly welcome sleep!

THE PILGRIM.

How so? 'Tis surely bliss for any man
To live and gladden in so sweet a place?

ADAM.

I know not. Times are changed. In times gone by,
When Fever and Disease and Pestilence
Walk'd freely through the streets and garner'd men,
I have mark'd upon the brows of those that died
A light that comes not now. I have stood and watch'd
By deathbeds, and as Death bent down to grasp
The throbbing throat and clutch the fluttering life,
I have seen him shrink and like a frighten'd hound
Crouch panting at the flash o' the dying face,
The proud imperious wave o' the dying hand;
Yea oftentimes, when men call'd out on God,

Defying Death with smiles, it seem'd a charm
To affright the Phantom which affrighteth all!

THE PILGRIM.

Yet now men welcome Death, as thou hast said.

ADAM.

Yea, but how differently, how wearily!
With no sweet hope of waking, with no thought
Of meeting those who have fallen to sleep before;
With no glad childish vision of delight
To come upon them when the morrow breaks
Happy and loving as a father's face.
They know their day is o'er, and that is all:
What matter if it hath been sunny and merry,
'Tis ended—night come duly—all is done.
Moreover, now-a-days, methinks that men,
Knowing so clearly, love not one another
As in the good old times when I was young!
For, look you, master, wedlock is a bond
Between the strong and strong, who know that soon
All fall asunder in Death's crucible;
And when a man or woman dies by chance,
What use to mourn?—the vase of life is broken,

And there's an end; wherefore, methinks, that
    men
Knew more of Love when they were mournfuller.
For Suffering and Sorrow walk'd the world
Like veiléd angels pointing heavenward,
And folk were sadder then, but hopefuller;
And now, indeed, since Hope hath gone away
With all the other angels, Death alone
Remains the one cold friend and comforter.

Now much I marvell'd, hearing such sad speech
Drop from the old man's mouth like simple sooth;
And gazing down upon the glorious City
Which sparkled in the sunshine under us,
Seeing the earth and air alive with life,
And catching from afar the faint glad cries
Of multitudinous creatures fluttering
Like motes in the sunbeam, still I seem'd to be
A ghost upon the borderland of Death,
Having no portion in humanity;
And like another ghost the old man seem'd,
Garrulously babbling with a voice as thin
As any heard in dream; then side by side
We walk'd together to the highest bourne
Of that fair burial-place, and lo! I saw,
Stretching before me on the further side,

A darkness like a mighty thunder-cloud—
Darkness on darkness, far as eye could see.

'What land lies yonder at our feet?' I said,
And pointed downward. Gravely he replied:
' Nay, sir, I know not, but I have heard folk say
A melancholy and a sunless land,
Forest on forest, dreary, without bound,—
Haunted by monsters, beasts and saurians
Of the primæval slime ; a land, alack !
Unfit for man to dwell in, melancholy
As were the dusk beginnings of the world.'

Then in my dream, which seem'd no dream at all,
Methought I leapt, like one who takes the plunge
From some black cape into a midnight sea,
Into that gulf of darkness ; and the night
Crash'd round and o'er me, as I sunk and sunk
Down, down, to dark oblivion deep as death ;
When for a space I lost all count of time,
But senseless lay amid the ooze and drift
Of the unconscious shadows ; yet at last
I stirr'd and waken'd, lying like a weed
On a cold isle of moonlight in the midst
Of cloud on cloud breaking like wave on wave
Around me ; thro' the darkness I perceived

Far off the glowworm glimmer of the City
Which I had left behind.
                        Feebly I rose,
Affrighted at the cold new stir of life
Along my veins, and murmur'd, 'Woe is me!
I live, who would have died; I am quick, who fain
Would have return'd to stony nothingness!
And I have search'd the world, and left the prints
Of my sad footsteps on the tracts of Time,
Yet am I houseless and a wanderer still
From City unto City, knowing at last
My quest is fruitless and my dreaming vain!'

Then with a cry I faced the seas of night,
And blindly hasten'd on, I knew not whither!

BOOK XV.

THE CELESTIAL OCEAN.

METHOUGHT I pass'd into the shadowy land
Where Nature like a gorgon mother sits
Devouring her own young; a rocky land,
Formless, chaotic, lonely, terrible,
And yet alive with monstrous shapes as strange
As e'er mad poet fabled : shapes that lived,
And moan'd, and open'd jaws chimæra-like,
And changed, and died; yet ever when I sought
To approach them, faded into lifeless forms
Of crag and rock. In stagnant sunless meres
I saw foul monsters swim, some serpent-wise,
Others web-footed like the water-birds,
While overhead, from a black mountain-peak,
The wingéd pterodactyl of the chalk
Flapt to its eyrie on the snake-strewn shore.
'Almighty God,' I moan'd, 'whose Hand did frame
These hideous creatures of the ooze and slime,
Within whose lineaments I seem to trace

Strange far-off hints of sweeter shapes and forms
Flowering at last in naked flesh of man,
Haunt me not with the deathlike fantasy
Of pageants fit for Hell!' And as I spake
Meseem'd I felt within my living veins
The speckled blood that steals like quicksilver
Under the hydra's skin, and knew my sense
Sick with primæval foulness of the slime
From which 'twas fashion'd when the Monster ruled
A rank and watery world. Yet I beheld
Within that land of portents pale gray men
Who stood and smiled, as happy children smile
On curious gnomes and trolls of Faeryland;
And many murmur'd, 'Wondrous is the Lord!
Whose word hath touch'd the darkness, till, behold,
It stirs and breathes and lives!'
        How long I walk'd
In that wild realm I know not, but at last
I found myself ascending a steep path
Upwinding to forlornest mountain-peaks;
And as I went the light grew cheerfuller,
And far away above my head I saw
A light clear space of sun-kist snow that seem'd
Like God's hand resting on the Mastodon
That felt it and was still; and suddenly
There flew across my path a bright-eyed bird

Of eagle-size, but whiter than a dove,
And fluttering upward lighted on a rock
And waved its pinions looking down upon me,
And when I follow'd rose and fled again,
Again alighting; thus from rock to rock
It flew, I following, while at every step
The light grew clearer, and my soul less sad.

At last methought I reach'd a green plateau
Far up among the peaks and loud with sound
Of many torrents falling; and the grass
That grew thereon was strewn with tiny shells,
Prismatic, beautiful, left by the lips
Of some receding sea; and pausing there,
I gazed into the valleys I had quitted,
And saw a darkness as of flood and cloud
Spear'd by the red lance of the setting sun,
And from the darkness came a solemn sound,
Terrible, elemental, as of waves
Wandering without a home.
                              While thus I stood,
I saw two shapes approaching from the peaks,
One leading and one following: that, a child,
Bright as a sunbeam, merry and golden-hair'd,
Who ran before and beckon'd, ran again
And beckon'd pausing; this, a reverent man,

Clad in a robe of samite white as snow,
And leaning on a staff enwrought with shapes
Of flower and dove and serpent. As they came
Great awe fell on me, for methought 'They come
To bring me tidings that my search is done!'
Fair was that Child, and 'neath her rosy feet
The coarse grass blossom'd into crystal blooms,
And fair was he who follow'd reverently—
Most proud his step as if he walk'd on thrones,
His dark eyes suffering with the kingly light
They shed upon me through his reverend hair.

And coming near, the Child with birdlike cries
Paused, looking on my features wonderingly,
Then turning quickly beckon'd once again,
And slowly approaching he who follow'd her
Did greet me like a monarch welcoming
Some stranger to the kingdom which he rules;
Then looking on my pilgrim's staff and scrip,
And pouring into my half-dazzled eyes
Strange lustre of his own dark orbs, he said:
'Welcome, O Stranger, to these lonely peaks!
Far hast thou travell'd from a weary world
To find firm foothold on the mountains here.'
And as he spake he placed his gentle hand
Upon the bright head of the Child, who stood

Smiling and listening; and his voice was deep
As torrent-voices partly drowning it,
Yet musical and passionately calm.

THE PILGRIM.

Far have I travell'd, wearily have I sought
A world of sense and phantoms, shapes and signs,—
Since in an earthly City last I stood
Wailing my lot and calling out on God.

THE MAN.

Be comforted—here shall thy cry be still'd,
Or drown'd in voices more miraculous.
Thou comest from the City where I was born?

THE PILGRIM.

The City men have builded, without God?

THE MAN.

The same. These hands of mine did help to raise
Some of its temples, and its inmost shrine.
When I drew breath 'twas but a noxious marsh
With some few dwellings long untenanted,
But in the heyday of my youth I cried:
'Upbuild! create a City out of stone

That we who know not God may dwell therein;'
Saying moreover, 'Wiser far are they
Who drain the marsh and make the market thrive
Than they who waste their toil on pyramids.'
Ev'n while I spake the City of Man upgrew,
To music sweet of the invisible choir
Who form the dusky vanguard of the dead;
And temples rose like lilies from the mere
Of human creatures multitudinous,
And Night was vanquish'd, and Disease and Pain
Crept from the shining of the strange new light.

The Pilgrim.

But Death remain'd.

The Man.

    And reign'd! Ere long I saw
The Shadow veil'd with sunlight looking down
Upon the beauteous City we had built;
And with a spectral hand he pointed ever
At the glad pageant, at the heart of man,
And at the living soul within the soul.
Then thought I, 'Man hath conquer'd God, not Death,
And the broad harvest Man hath sown, Death reaps;'

And surely I had madden'd in despair,
Had I not seen one morning, as I stood
In the still burial-place beyond the City,
This Child, who ran and play'd among the tombs,
Blown hither and thither like a butterfly
By some strange wind of gladness; then behold,
She beckon'd, and I follow'd (for methought
She was not as the common things of earth,
But wondrous, fed on some diviner air);
And from the gates she drew me with a smile
Until I came, as thou thyself didst come,
Among the darkness of primæval Time,
Haunted by monsters, hydras, mastodons,
Strange forms, the slime of Chaos; but whene'er
I falter'd faint of heart, the Child ran back
And slipt her little hand into mine own,
And prattling of the sunshine and the dawn
Did draw me gently on, until at last
I left the haunted valleys and beheld
A stainless snow like to the hand of God
Lying on yonder peaks; and even yet
I know not if the thing that led me on,
And leads me ever, is a mortal Child,
Or some angelic presence sent to guide
My footsteps through the shadows of the world.

THE PILGRIM.

An angel, surely! See how rapturously
Her happy face is shining into thine!
An angel still, if human; for methinks
Her eyes reflect the glory and the dream
Of God's celestial City which I seek.
Yet surely this is evil, that thy feet
Still tread the loneness of the mountain-tops,
Thine eyes see not the splendour she hath seen?

THE MAN.

It is enough to know that such things are,
Beyond the silence and the setting sun.

THE PILGRIM.

Alas! how knowest thou not that after all
They are not phantasies and images
Like those that met thee yonder in the vales?
Alas! if thou hast won these lonely heights,
What hast thou gain'd, what have thy soul's eyes seen
More than the souls in yonder City see?

THE MAN.

The peace of God, the assurance of His heaven,
Seen mirror'd in the blue eyes of a Child!

The Pilgrim.
But surely Death shall follow and find thee here?

The Man.
I wait his coming, eager for more light
Such as he brings to those who love its beams,
Yet not impatient, for from these high peaks
I look on more than mortal sight can measure
Or human soul conceive and apprehend:
Dawn flying like a dove from isle to isle
Of Chaos; infinite and wondrous life
Stirring from form to form; the march of lives
From sleep to sleep, from death to death; the flow
Of earth's progressions, and the ebb of Time.
Wherefore mine age is clothed with mastery
As with a garment; slowly I have learn'd
That to be young and innocent is best,
Next best it is to be serene and old.

The Pilgrim.
Having beheld these things, beholding still
Their stress and pain, dost thou believe on God?

The Man.
I know not. What is infinite transcends

The seeing of the finite, evermore.
Gaze in the heavenly eyes of this fair Child,
And thou shalt see a light more mystical
Than all thy spirit can conceive of God.
Pilgrim of earth, wouldst thou behold a sign?
Conceive the inconceivable, attain
To prescience which would prove, if absolute,
The annihilation of thy thinking soul?
Come, then, and standing yonder on the
    peaks,
The highest point of earth, survey the waste
Of that mysterious Ocean without bound,
Which wash'd thee hither as a grain of sand
And sow'd thee deep among these drifts of dust
To quicken into strange humanity!

He ceased; and on the heights above his head
The daylight faded, while the hand of Night
Hung closed a moment o'er the rayless
    snows,
Then open'd suddenly and from its grasp
Loosen'd one lustrous star! Then with a cry
The Child sprang upward on the dizzy path,
And paused above us beckoning; and we
    follow'd
From crag to crag till we together stood

Close to the edge of that celestial Sea
Which breaks for ever on these dark shores of earth.

Lone on the heights we stood as on a strand
Oceanward gazing; and the world beneath
Faded to an abyss of nothingness,
Unseen, unheard, unknown, but at our feet
The waves of ether rippled, gleam'd, and broke
In silence; and as far as eye could see
The waste cœrulean stretch'd in windless calm,
Here bright, there shadowy, strewn with shimmering
    flakes
Like lunar gleams; and suddenly, to lend
New splendour to the solitary scene,
The island of the moon broke into beams
And shook upon the azure shallows around
Wild shafts of silver: then the stillness grew
Intenser, and the deep ethereal voids
Seem'd opening to their inmost, till I saw
Far as the pin-point of the furthest sphere
In the dark silence and abysm of space,
And from the far-off unimagined shores
There came, or seem'd to come, a stir of sound
So faint it scarce did seem to touch the sleep
Of that vast Ocean!
                Then with reverent eyes

Up-gazing, and upon his pallid face
Light falling faintly from a million worlds,
Thus spake that old man masterful, my guide:

' Thou seekest God—behold thou standest now
Within His Temple. Lo, how brilliantly
The Altar, fed with ceaseless starry fires,
Burns, for its footstool is the mountain-peaks,
The skies its star-enwoven panoply!—
Lo, then, how silently, how mystically,
Yonder unsullied Moon uplifts the Host,
While from the continents and seas beneath,
And from the planets that bow down as lambs,
And from the constellations clustering
With eyes of wonder upon every side,
Rises the murmur which Creation heard
In the beginning! Hearken! Strain thine ears!
Are they so thick with dust they cannot hear
The plagal cadence of the instrument
Set in the veiléd centre of the Shrine!'

He ceased, with arms outstretch'd to the great Deep
In adoration; and once more I seem'd
To catch that music, rather felt than heard,
Out of the open'd heavens; and lo, it grew
Deeper, intenser, audible as breath,

With thrills as from the silvern stops of stars
And murmurous constellations!

       ' Hearken yet!'
He murmur'd, while I trembled to my knees,
' Yonder the veil'd Musician sits, his feet
Upon the pedals of dark formless suns,
His fingers on the radiant spheric keys,
His face, that it is death to look upon,
Misted with incense rising nebulous
Out of abysmal chaos and cohering
Into the golden flames of Life and Being!
And underneath his touch Music itself
Grows living, heard as far as thought can creep
Or dream can soar; so that Creation stirs,
And drinks the sound, and sings!—So far
  away
He sits, the Mystery, wrapt for ever round
With brightness and with awe and melody;
Yet even here, on these low-lying shores,
Lower than is the footstool of His throne,
We hear Him and adore Him, nay, can feel
His breath as vapour round our mouths, inhaling
That soul within the soul whereby we live
From that divine for-ever-beating Heart
Which thrills the universe with Light and Love!'

The Pilgrim.

So far away He dwells, my soul indeed
Scarcely discerns him, and in sooth I seek
A gentler Presence and a nearer Friend.

The Man.

So far? O blind, He broods beside thee now
Here in this silence, with His eyes on Thine!
O deaf, His voice is whispering in thine ears
Soft as the breathing of the slumberous seas!

The Pilgrim.

I see not and I hear not; but I see
Thine eyes burn dimly, like a corpse-light seen
Flickering amidst the tempest; and I hear
Only the elemental grief and pain
Out of whose shadow I would creep for ever.

The Man.

Thou canst not, brother; for these, too, are God!

The Pilgrim.

How? Is my God, then, as a homeless ghost
Blown this way, that way, with the elements?

THE MAN.

He is without thee, and within thee, too;
Thy living breath, and that which drinks thy breath;
Thy being, and the bliss beyond thy being.

THE PILGRIM.

So near, so far? He shapes the furthest sun
New-glimmering on the furthest fringe of space,
Yet stoops and with a leaf-light finger-touch
Reaches my heart and makes it come and go!

THE MAN.

Yea; and He is thy heart within thy heart,
And thou a portion of His Heart Divine!

THE PILGRIM.

Alas! what comfort comes to grief like man's
To weave a circle of sweet fantasy
Around him, and to share so dim a dream?
For if thy calm philosophy be true,
He is, yet is not, here; breathes with our breath,
Yet evermore eludes us like the stir
Of the unconscious life within our veins;
Haunts us for ever in a mystery,

Broods close within us 'tween our walls of flesh,
Yet when we seek to look into His eyes
Fades far away above us and looks down
With loveless eyes of stars.   Meantime my quest
Is for a City builded on the rock,
Not on the raincloud; for a God whose face
Is humanised to lineaments of love;
Not one who, when my hand would clutch His robe,
Slips as a flash of light from world to world
And fades from form to form, then vanishes
Back to the formless sense within my soul
Which evermore pursues and loses Him!

E'en as I spake methought (so strangely changed
My wondrous dream that was no dream at all)
That not alone we stood on those dark shores,
But round us gather'd ghostly living forms
Featured like men and women, pointing hands
Out to the dusky space and starry isles;
And on the sands below them silent lay
Two bright transparent forms as if asleep—
One old and hoary, featured like a man,
The other maidenlike and golden-hair'd;
And o'er these sleeping, smiling as they slept,
That radiant Child bent tearfully and cried,
'Awake, awake!' but they awaken'd not,

Though quietly the lucent waves of light
Crept near and rippled round their shrouded feet.

Then said aloud that old man masterful:
'They are not dead but sleeping,—vex them not,
Their eyes shall open on serener shores.
We come from the eternal night to find,
And not to lose, each other; what is born
And liveth cannot die.[1]   And while those forms
Still pointing wildly seaward moan'd and sobb'd,
He murmur'd, 'Ere these twain lay down and
　　　slept,
They pray'd the prayer and sang the song which
　　　Man
Hath made from the beginning.   Sing it *now*,
That He who listens through eternity
Yonder across the azure seas may hear.'

And lo, methought, in piteous human tones
Those spirits bent above the dead and sang :—

　　　Unseen, Unknown, yet seen and known
　　　By the still soul that broods alone
　　　　　　On visions eyesight cannot see,
　　　By that, thy seed within me sown,
　　　　　　Forget not me!

The Celestial Ocean.

Forget me not, but hear me cry,
Ere in my lonely bed I lie,
  Thus stooping low on bended knee,
And if in glooms of sleep I die,
  Forget not me!

Forget me not as men forget,
But let thy light be with me yet
  Where'er my vagrant footsteps flee,
Until my earthly sun is set,
  Forget not me!

Though dumb thou broodest far away,
Beyond the night, beyond the day,
  Across the great celestial Sea,
Forget me not, but hear me pray
  'Forget not me!'

By the long path that I have trod,
The sunless tracks, the shining road,
  From forms of dread to forms of Thee,
By all my dumb despairs, O God,
  Forget not me!

Forget not when mine eyelids close,
And sinking to my last repose,
  All round the sleeping dead I see,
Yea, when I sleep as sound as those,
  Forget not me!

> Forget me not as they forget,
> Hush'd from the fever and the fret,
> From all long life's remembrance free,
> Though I forget, remember yet—
> Forget not me!

Then even as they sang meseem'd I saw
Far off upon the rippling waves of light
A shadowy Bark approaching with no sound,
Wing'd like an eagle, floating ominously
On that aërial sea; from space to space
Of brightness, and from shadow on to shadow,
It moved, until at last its shining prow
Touch'd the dusk shore, and paused; and in it sat
A Spirit dark and hooded, girt around
With many shining forms,—and not on these
The Spirit gazed, nor on the shapes that throng'd
The sands of earth, but on the spectral faces
Of that worn hoary man and gold-hair'd maid
Who lay there waiting, smiling in their shrouds.

Then as the very heart within me fail'd,
And on that sight I gazed through blinding tears,
The old man stretching white hands heaven'ward
Cried: 'Lo, the life which ends and but begins!
God that remembers, Death that ne'er forgets,
The dream of generations justified!

O Grave, where is thy victory! O Death,
Where is thy sting! O deathless Mystery,
At last we apprehend and sleep in peace!
For this the timorous nebulæ cohered
To fashion luminous worlds; for this the night
Conceived and labour'd, till the infant Life
Quicken'd within its womb and stirr'd and lived;
For this all things have striven and agonized,
Flashing from ever-changing form to form,
Yet, as the flame ascending clarifies,
Growing for ever purer, peacefuller,
Till that divinest growth, the Soul of Man,
Was fashion'd paramount and stood supreme,
And trembling with the very breath it drew
Knowing itself, beheld within itself
The inspiration it hath christen'd "God,"
And which *alone* betokens it divine!'

Then, as he spake, methought that radiant Child
Approach'd him, knelt, with eyes divinely glad
Look'd up in his, and all the seas of heaven
Kindled and brighten'd, while with outstretch'd arms
Of blessing, drinking in with rapturous gaze
The splendour of the radiant universe,
The old man cried:
    'O Mystery Divine,

Simple as babble of the yeanling babes,
And gentle as the breath of mother's love!
How far we seek thee o'er these wastes of
    Time,
And find thee not, although thou broodest ever
Within us, like an ever-homing dove!
Nay, all we see, upon these luminous walls
Of sense conditioning and surrounding us,
Is what thine Eldest-born and Best-beloved
Saw long ago,—a crimson cross of pain,
A cipher which whoever reads hath read
The riddle of the worlds. And Man hath raised
City on city, creed on creed, hath sought
To chain the electric lightnings of the soul
In temple upon temple, all in vain;
Yet what he found not visibled in form
Hath haunted him with dreams invisible
From height to height, till like a god he stands
Perceiving good and evil, knowing himself
Thine effluence, and immortal. Thus the law
Within him, yet without him, justifies
The eternal law he cannot understand
Yet drinks like royal breath; and all his pain
Falls from him like a garment, leaving him
Naked and warm in light, a happy child
Sure of his birthright, innocent and wise,

Foredoom'd to that eternal hope and joy
Whose other names are God, and Life, and Love!'

Aye me, the tearful wonder of my dream!
For shapes of brightness raised those twain who
    slept
And placed them in the Bark, when through their
    frames
The crystal splendour of eternity
Shot sacramental; and the hooded Spirit
Bent o'er the dead, and his dim eyes distill'd
Bright tears like dew, while all those shining
    shapes
Gather'd around and sang the same sweet hymn
Which those had sung who throng'd the lonely shore.

    Though deeper than the deepest Deep
    Be the dark void wherein I sleep,
        Though ocean-deep I buried be,
    I charge Thee, by these tears I weep,
        Forget not me!

    Remember, Lord, my lifelong quest,
    How painfully my soul hath prest
        From dark to light, pursuing Thee;
    So, though I fail and sink to rest,
        Forget not me!

Say not 'He sleeps—he doth forget
All that he sought with eyes tear-wet—
    'Tis o'er—he slumbers—let him be!'
Though *I* forget, remember yet—
    Forget not me!

Forget me not, but come, O King,
And find me softly slumbering
    In dark and troubled dreams of Thee—
Then, with one waft of Thy bright wing,
    Awaken me!

Then lost in wonder, standing on that shore,
The highest peak of earth, I sigh'd aloud:
'Yea, God remembers, God can ne'er forget! . . .
I have gone inland and not oceanward—
The earthly Cities only have I known—
But these who sleep shall waken and behold,
Yonder across those wastes whereon they sail,
God and the radiant City of my Dream!'

And as I spake the ether at my feet
Broke, rippling amethystine. Far away
The mighty nebulous Ocean, where the spheres
Pass'd and repass'd like golden argosies,
Grew phosphorescent to its furthest depths:
Light answer'd light, star flash'd to star, and space,
As far away as the remotest sun

Small as the facet of a diamond,
Sparkled; and from the ethereal Deep there rose
The breath of its own being and the stir
Of its own rapture. Then to that strange sound
Stiller than silence, the pale Ship of Souls
Moved from the shore; I stood and watch'd it steal
From pool to pool of light, from shade to shade,
Then melting into splendour fade away
Amid the haze of those cœrulean seas.

L'ENVOI.

ὦ θάνατε παιάν.

O BLESSÈD Death! O white-wing'd form,
    Still winging through the night!
O Dove, that seekest through the storm
    Some lonely Ark of Light!

While the dark flood of human pain
    Rises with weariest moans,
Touching and falling back again
    From heaven's deserted thrones,

Thou wanderest on with wondrous wings
    On that celestial quest!
And looking on thee, weary things
    Sob tearfully and rest!

What were the world and what were Man
    Without thee, heavenly Death?
An empty sky, a starless span,
    A mist of troubled breath!

The one thing sure, the one thing pure,
    The one thing all divine,
Though all else ceases, doth endure,
    Though all grows dark, doth shine!

Our souls have probed this world of clay,
    And measured the great sea,
Our sight hath conquer'd night and day,
    But still thou soarest free!

Wisdom hath cried, 'No God! not one!
  Nay, heaven and earth shall cease!'
But as thou passest, winging on,
  We hush our cries in peace.

For all things fade, save thou alone,
  Bird of the sleepless wing!
From world to world, from zone to zone,
  We see thee voyaging!

Angel of God, still homeless here,
  Now clouds have hid God's face,—
Bright Dove that on these waves of fear
  Can find no resting-place!

O blessèd Death,—O Angel fair,
  Still keep thy course divine!
Till o'er the flood of our despair
  The Bow of God doth shine!

A PROSE NOTE.

A PROSE NOTE.

I HAVE called the *City of Dream* an epic poem, using the term in a new and somewhat unfamiliar sense, and believing it applicable to any poetical work which embodies, in a series of grandiose pictures, the intellectual spirit of the age in which it is written. The *Iliad* and *Odyssey* are the epic, or epoch, poems of the heroic or pagan period; the *De Rerum Natura* is the epic of Roman scepticism and decadence; the *Divine Comedy* is the epic of Roman Catholicism, the *Paradise Lost* that of the epoch known as Protestant; Bunyan's *Pilgrim's Progress* (as surely a poem, although written in prose, as any of those others) is the epic of English Dissent; while, to compare small things with great, the *City of Dream* is an epic of modern Revolt and Reconciliation. My book, indeed, attempts to be, for the inquiring modern spirit, what the lovely vision of Bunyan is for those who still exist in the fairyland of dogmatic Christianity; but dealing, as it must, with elements more complex and indeterminate, touching on problems which to the orthodox believer do not even exist, it is necessarily less matter-of-fact, and in all probability less sufficing. Be that as it may, the sympathetic modern will find here the record of his own heartburnings, doubts, and experiences, though they may not have occurred to him in the same order or culminated in the same way; though he may not have passed through the Valley of Dead Gods at all, or looked with wondering eyes on the Spectre of the Inconceivable; though he may never have realised to the full, as I have done, the existence of the City without God, or have come at last, footsore and despairing, to find solace and certainty on the brink of the Celestial Ocean.

To the orthodox believer in Christianity there is but one righteous Book, the Old and New Testaments. To the present writer all books are righteous which, in one way or another, help the soul on its heavenward pilgrimage, sound the depths of spiritual speculation, and habituate the ear of conscience to the harmonies of some higher and more perfect life. The reader will therefore find, figured in the foregoing pages, many of those divine teachers who seem, to some of us, superior to most Saints in the Calendar. The entire poem represents the thought and speculation of many years. How much has been attempted may be seen in such a section as that of 'The Amphitheatre,' where an effort is made to adumbrate the entire spirit of Greek poetry and theology. No man can live entirely in the past; but a modern poet must at least have paused in it and learned to love it, before he is competent to offer any interpretation, however faltering, of the problems of religion, literature, and life.

For the form and style of the work I shall make no apology. It illustrates once more the theory of poetical expression that has guided me throughout my career,—the theory that the end and crown of Art is simplicity, and that words, where they only conceal thought, are the veriest weeds, to be cut remorselessly away. If there is mysticism anywhere in the book (and I hope there is very little) it is assuredly not in the mere words. But in the present generation a poet who deals with Divine issues must be prepared for the neglect of the idle and the misconstruction of the impatient.

ROBERT BUCHANAN.

PR   Buchanan, Robert Williams
4262   The city of dream
C5
1888

PLEASE DO NOT REMOVE
CARDS OR SLIPS FROM THIS POCKET

UNIVERSITY OF TORONTO LIBRARY

www.ingramcontent.com/pod-product-compliance
Lightning Source LLC
Chambersburg PA
CBHW030405230426
43664CB00007BB/765